"Finally, my friend Benny Tate has put ... turned life's test into a testimony, and he gives you principles ... you can do it too! Each chapter is personal, practical, and powerful! I read the first chapter and was hooked. You will be as well!"

John C. Maxwell,
author and founder of the John Maxwell Team,
the John Maxwell Co., and EQUIP Leadership

"It's my great privilege to recommend the book *Defy the Odds* by my dear friend Benny Tate. From the very beginning of his life, even until now, he has by the grace of God defied the odds at every turn. No matter how helpless or hopeless you may think your situation is, if you read this book you will be convinced otherwise. I cannot commend it too highly."

James Merritt,
host of *Touching Lives*, senior pastor of Cross Pointe Church,
former president of the Southern Baptist Convention

"Talk about an underdog. What are the chances or the odds? Yet God! In His mercy, He took Benny Tate's mess and performed a miracle. Need hope? It's in the pages of this book!"

Johnny Hunt,
senior vice president Evangelism/Pastoral Leadership,
North American Mission Board,
former president Southern Baptist Convention,
pastor emeritus First Baptist Church, Woodstock, Georgia

"Pastor Benny speaks wisdom in practical ways we can grasp and apply to our own lives. His message is authentic because he has lived it in his own life. He doesn't preach from a lofty tower; he wasn't born in a pulpit. His life had a dreadful beginning, but he chose to surrender his life fully to the One who had a good plan for his life—Jesus Christ. This is his story."

Ruth Graham,
author of *Forgiving My Father, Forgiving Myself*

"Whatever or whoever is standing in your way will be removed from your life! How can I say that? If God can do that for my friend Benny Tate, He will do the same for you. *Defy the Odds* may just be the most transparent and transformative book you will read. Not only will you read it, you will want all those you love to read it too. I've known Pastor Benny Tate for many years, and reading this book only increased my respect, admiration, and honor for him."

Sam Chand,
leadership consultant and author of *Harnessing the Power of Tension*

"Pastor Benny Tate's story is one of both inspiration and faith. The guy who starts on third base, gets home, and acts as though he hit a home run has never impressed me. My good friend Pastor Tate not only didn't start on third base, he wasn't even in the stadium. His life is proof that if you have faith and the right mindset and belief, you can truly do anything and defy all odds."

John Calipari,
head coach, University of Kentucky men's basketball

"Benny Tate is no stranger to adversity and heartache. However, his story is a perfect example of how God can overcome every difficult circumstance and use anyone regardless of their past. This book offers hope to all who read it! Each chapter provides practical application for believing God for big things and trusting Him to defy the odds in your life."

Dr. Robert Jeffress,
senior pastor, First Baptist, Dallas, Texas

"This story of a brave young man from an ungodly background with the courage to defy the odds as a pastor and leader is a challenge to every Christian to stand firm in the faith."

Mrs. Adrian (Joyce) Rogers,
author and board member of Love Worth Finding Ministries

"*Defy the Odds* by my friend Benny Tate will strengthen your faith in the fact that with God, all things are possible!"

Jim Cymbala,
pastor, Brooklyn Tabernacle

"Benny Tate's life could have turned out much differently, but he made the decision to break the chains that had imprisoned his family legacy. Through incredible storytelling, harrowing true stories, and pinpoint biblical truths, Benny teaches how readers can defy the odds and overcome the struggles and challenges of this broken world."

Reverend Will Graham,
vice president, Billy Graham Evangelistic Association

"I was not prepared for how much I would enjoy Benny Tate's book. When I finished, I asked myself, *Is this not the most encouraging book I have ever read?* If you have felt you were born with all good possibilities completely against you, this is the book for you. If you feel there is no hope, this is your book. If you feel life has been unfair to you, this is your book. God has raised up Benny Tate to demonstrate to the world what God can do with the most impossible situation. Benny Tate also happens to be a gifted writer, which will make this book easy reading for you. If you are ready to be uplifted, start reading now!"

R.T. Kendall,
Christian writer, speaker, teacher,
and 25-year-pastor of Westminster Chapel

"Benny Tate's story is one of pain and triumph. It's a real-life exhibit of 2 Corinthians 1, where the apostle Paul tells us that the help you have received in your tough times allows you to help others. *Defy the Odds* brings help and hope to people's lives."

Tim Dilena,
senior pastor of Times Square Church, New York City

"Overcoming life's greatest obstacles is impossible on your own, but with God, all things are possible. *Defy the Odds* paints a wonderful picture of how God can use any person regardless of their past mistakes or difficult circumstances. If you need to be reminded that God can use you to accomplish great things, Benny Tate's story will encourage you to trust that God can transform your life in unimaginable ways!"

Roma Downey,
Emmy*-nominated actress, producer,
and *New York Times* bestselling author

"If you meet Benny Tate, the words within these pages become all the more miraculous. It's not only his accomplishments, which are many. It's not just the people who love him, which are even more. It's his attitude and spirit, and it's his willingness to help you reach your own destiny any way he can. That's the most miraculous of all."

Todd Tilghman,
recording artist and winner of season 18 of NBC's *The Voice*

DEFY

THE

ODDS

BENNY TATE
WITH BRITTANY MCKNEELY

HARVEST HOUSE PUBLISHERS
EUGENE, OREGON

Cover design by Faceout Studio

Cover photo © cepera / Shutterstock

Interior design by KUHN Design Group

For bulk, special sales, or ministry purchases, please call 1-800-547-8979.
Email: Customerservice@hhpbooks.com

Defy the Odds
Copyright © 2022 by Benny Tate
Published by Harvest House Publishers
Eugene, Oregon 97408
www.harvesthousepublishers.com

ISBN 978-0-7369-8509-3 (pbk.)
ISBN 978-0-7369-8510-9 (eBook)

Library of Congress Control Number: 2021937786

To my wife, Barbara

Without you there would be no book—
you believed in it long before I ever did.
You have always been my biggest supporter,
and I believe many of the amazing things
God has allowed me to do have been because
of your prayers over the years. You are
my greatest blessing, and I love you!

CONTENTS

◆

FOREWORD

It's rare to find a pastor who is as comfortable in front of corporate giants and US senators as he is with his own congregation. Whether he's speaking to executives at Delta Air Lines, ServiceMaster, or Chick-fil-A or to his own congregation, Benny has a way of relating core scriptural values and principles that transcend titles and stations in life, all in such a way that people are truly inspired to take action and create change.

Defy the Odds takes you behind the curtain and offers life lessons forged in the pain and triumph Benny has experienced. As you walk through these chapters, you will see how God's plan and His hand were on Benny long before he was born. Then at each stage of Benny's life, the Lord positioned a caregiver to provide him with timely direction as He shaped him for a purpose he never could have imagined.

I believe you will find yourself in the space between the lines because Benny's struggles were not unlike struggles we all face. Yours may have a different name or take place in a different context, but your life's challenges are not as unique to you as you may believe. What is unique is God's plan for each of us. That is made clear in every story and teaching in this book.

Each chapter offers a fresh perspective for every season of your life, building a foundation of hope for all your tomorrows. You can defy the odds simply because you carry the very presence of God into every situation you face and every ministry opportunity you encounter. *Defy the Odds* will show you how to maintain hope in all circumstances, as only a master communicator like Benny can do.

Through surrender and sacrifice, Benny has a way of turning the most unlikely circumstance into something amazing. Whether successfully navigating the scholarly world as a guest speaker on college campuses or growing a young church of 50 people into a church of more than 8,000, Benny has discovered a hidden pathway to success and victory. He is incredibly passionate about sharing that path with whoever is willing to sit and listen—or in this case, willing to sit and read.

I promise you this: Whatever situation you find yourself in today—rich or poor, highly successful or just trying to get on your feet—God has so much more for you. *Defy the Odds* will show you, step by step and story by story, how to walk in all He has for your life. Benny's story begins before he was even born, and you, too, will discover that your journey isn't just about finding your next step or making that next decision but also about learning that you have been a part of God's plan before you ever took a breath.

You, my friend, were made for more, and it's time to start defying the odds in your own life!

Jentezen Franklin,
senior pastor of Free Chapel and
New York Times bestselling author

THE NEED FOR HOPE

I f you had observed the first 16 years of my life, you might have found it hard to believe I'd become a preacher. You might have thought it more probable that I'd be thrown into prison before I hit 19, assuming I didn't end up dead long before then. You might have thought the odds were stacked against me so high that I'd never be able to overcome them, never have a family, never have much of anything to offer the world let alone to God. And you wouldn't have been alone in that assessment.

Judge Nelson Layne was a superior court judge from my hometown who knew me and my family well when I was growing up. After I'd been preaching for many years, Judge Lane attended a service one Sunday and stopped at the door to shake my hand as he left. He said, "I always knew you'd stand before me one day. I just didn't know it would be in a pulpit."

While no one else expected much for my future, the Lord had different plans. I just had to surrender my life to Him. I had to allow Him to deal with the odds stacked against me from birth. I had to let Him guide me through the years ahead, and I had to cling to the hope I found in Him and Him alone. And when I did? I learned I could trust Him with my future.

I believe the average person struggles with trusting God with all that lies ahead in life. They may believe in God but struggle to believe there is *hope* in God, and that can make them fearful for their future. They're fearful because of concerns such as disease, terrorism, political unrest, and racial injustice, but they're also fearful because of challenging personal matters—perhaps financial insecurity, depression, addiction, a troubling or abusive relationship, or racial or other discrimination.

While all of these issues are legitimate concerns facing people in today's world, the odds of overcoming them only remain impossible in our own strength. When we determine in our hearts to keep our eyes on the Lord, the problems of this world seem much smaller. There is nothing our God cannot overcome, but we must believe in and hope in His power to overcome every obstacle.

A.W. Tozer once said of God, "All He has ever done for any of His children He will do for all of His children. The difference lies not with God but with us."[1] Tozer was right. God will do for His children now all that He has done for them in the past. The difference lies in us and the hope we have for the future because of His love, promises, and power.

Believing in God and trusting in God are not the same thing. Trust requires surrender. It requires you to lean into Him believing His promise to "uphold you with [His] righteous right hand" (Isaiah 41:10). My future changed when I chose to lean into God and trust Him with all of my tomorrows. Corrie ten Boom said it best: "Never be afraid to trust an unknown future to a known God."[2] You can trust God with all your tomorrows too.

You will find a section in the back of the book, "Leaning In, Digging Deeper," for you to take notes as you read through each chapter. There is also space for you to write a specific prayer for how you would like to see God defy the odds in your life. Friend, I hope you lean in and dig deep because I believe God is going to do a great work in your life as you read!

As I share the story of how the Lord has defied the odds in my life—as well as in Rock Springs Church and the lives of others—my prayer is that you will be encouraged to believe this truth: No matter what circumstances present overwhelming odds in your life, you can always hope in God for your future. He can defy the odds!

1

VICTOR OVER VICTIM

The pregnant, 20-year-old girl with fiery red hair and simple, worn clothes climbed into the car with the man she was dating, but she had no idea where they were headed as they rode in silence, his face hard and cold. The day was bleak with gray skies that offered no warmth, and the mood in the car mirrored the weather.

They pulled into the parking lot at a doctor's office, but it didn't look like a place anyone would willingly go for medical care. The building was old, and the signage out front was unprofessional. She thought perhaps the man she was with needed medical attention, and she was worried as she asked questions on their walk inside. "Are we here for you? Do you need to see a doctor?"

The man looked at her with grave seriousness and said, "No. This is not about me. I've set up something for *you*. You're going to abort that baby. You don't need it."

Much to her shock, everything was ready for her to walk right in and abort her child. She was scared. No one was going to kill her baby! But how could she afford to manage on her own now that she knew he had no intention of helping her?

She immediately ran out the door. No matter what she had to do, she would raise her child—me. Yes, her reality lacked a clear plan, steady resources, support, and education, but she was right not to take an innocent life even though the odds against her had just stacked a little higher. Mama wasn't a Christian, but I've always admired her for choosing me over an easier path.

You see, my mother had been battling the odds her entire life. She was raised in a dysfunctional home with abusive men, and she had only a sixth-grade education. Life was and had always been uphill for her. She could have gone through with the abortion that day and saved herself the trouble of struggling to make ends meet, but she didn't.

Here's the catcher: Not only was she only 20 years old and pregnant, but she already had a three-year-old daughter—my sister, Rhonda—whose father hadn't stuck around to fulfill his duties. And now she was pregnant again, and this man wasn't about to stick around either. *Two* little mouths to feed would certainly be more difficult, but all her choices in men had proven to be bad, and now the odds were stacked against her—again.

Overwhelming odds were stacked against me as well, obstacles littering the path my life was assumed to take. Yet God knew me and had a plan for my life long before I knew Him. I'm so glad He said in Jeremiah 1:5, "I knew you before I formed you in your mother's womb. Before you were born I set you apart" (NLT). I have always believed there may be accidental parents but no accidental children. God began defying the odds in my life long before I was born, and He continued defying them as they stacked against me higher and higher.

I was born on November 9, 1964. For the first 30 years of my life, I believed my biological father was Lee Tate. He and my mother married after I was born but soon parted ways after he adopted Rhonda and me. So it made sense that my name was Vincent Lynn *Tate*. I just didn't know Lee had adopted us. I also believed he died when I was very young. My mother wanted us to be like everyone else as much as possible and thought it better to let us believe our father was dead rather than us knowing the true character of our biological fathers.

Without Lee, Mama lived on her own with two small children. We had a tiny, one-bedroom apartment in McMinnville, Tennessee, and she worked two jobs—in a shirt factory by day and at a diner at night.

A friend of hers kept my sister while she was at work during the day and some nights, and she found someone else to care for me.

God Brings Jenny Travis

An old Pentecostal woman named Jenny Travis lived across the street from our apartment complex. Mamie, as I grew to call her, always wore her gray hair tied up in a bun and wore long dresses. I can't remember a time when she wasn't wearing long skirts, and she looked ready to head to church for Sunday service at any given moment. Her colored cardigans always matched her dress, and her large-framed glasses sat perched high on her nose. Mamie agreed to watch me while Mama was at work each day, but she had one issue to fix before I could stay with her. She said she couldn't pronounce the name Vincent, so she wanted to just call me Benny. From that moment on, I've been Benny Tate.

Mamie was a wonderful, godly woman the Lord used to defy the odds in my life. Later, she told me she would place her hands on me each day and pray, *God, You have a great plan for this baby. I want You to keep him safe. I know You're going to use this child in a very special way.* My mother wasn't a Christian and didn't know anything about praying, much less anything about praying blessings over her children, but God brought Mamie into my life and used her to pray blessings and favor over me. She prayed for provision over my life.

Mamie also told me all about Jesus long before I could walk or talk. Each day after my mother dropped me off, Mamie walked around the house showing me pictures of Jesus. Every room in her house had one on the wall. She would point and say, "Benny, that's Jesus." Then she'd point to another picture and say, "Benny, that's Jesus." And another. And another. Every single day she kept me, she pointed me to Jesus.

It came as no surprise to her or anyone else that my very first word was *Jesus*. You know, most children's first word is either *Mama* or *Dada*, but I had no father figure in my life, and my mother was working from morning to night. Mamie, being the godly woman she was, believed Proverbs 22:6: "Train up a child in the way he should go; even when he is old he will not depart from it." She used every opportunity she had to train me up in the way I should go by pointing me to Jesus. She didn't know the exact road I would travel in life, but she knew it would be a rough one.

I am so grateful that God positioned Mamie to be such an incredible influence on me during those formative years. She treated me just like her own. She even had photos of me hanging on the wall in her house along with photos of her own children and grandchildren.

I practically lived with her the first five years of my life, and to this day I attribute much of the provision and protection that have covered me throughout my life to those prayers Mamie was so faithful to pray. The odds may not have been in my favor, but I'm so glad the favor of God outweighs any odds that could ever be stacked against me.

It's funny how odds work—they're based on chance, likelihood, and probability. While odds might be useful in decision-making for gambling bets and buying and selling Wall Street stocks, they can't always be trusted to speak truth over someone's future. Odds are man-made, but there is nothing man-made about one's life.

When I was five years old, Mama came to Mamie's house to pick me up and said we were moving away. The only godly influence I had and all I knew to be home were taken from me that day, and my world was turned upside down. We packed our bags to move in with my mother's boyfriend, Bill—the very same man who had wanted to end my life before it began.

Ironically, we were moving to Shady Rest, Tennessee, but there was nothing restful or peaceful about living with Bill. Still, my mother chose to pursue a relationship with him because he was a man of some means, and she'd been struggling just to put food on the table for the three of us for a long time.

A Life of Abuse

Bill was a hard, vile man. He was abusive physically, mentally, verbally, and emotionally. Physically, he just didn't know when to quit with a belt; it wouldn't be anything for him to turn you over the bed and whip you so badly that you could hardly walk or sit down the next day.

One day when I was ten, Bill and I were out on his property, working on a fence. I hated helping him with chores—especially when we were alone. I always managed to do something wrong no matter how hard I tried to follow every detail of his instructions, and he consistently punished me really good for whatever mistake I made. That day I wasn't digging post holes exactly the way he liked, and he started throwing rocks at me while calling me terrible names. He hurled a rock and then hurled an insult. The insults hurt worse than the rocks.

He constantly called me an ignorant bastard and told me I would never amount to anything. Bill had children of his own, and he also regularly reminded Rhonda and me that we weren't his.

I would say the verbal abuse caused more long-term damage than the physical abuse, and by the time I was ten, the effects of the abuse had become noticeable in my mental state. Mama loaded Rhonda, me, and Bill's children into the car for our yearly physicals, but I didn't know until later in life that Mama actually wanted me evaluated for any kind of mental disability. I was having such a hard time learning in school.

The doctor said I didn't have a learning disability and there was nothing wrong with my mental state. I did, however, have a man in my life who daily told me I was stupid and couldn't learn. Words like that thrown at me for seven years became truth in my mind and were reflected in my academics.

James 3:6 is so true: "The tongue is a fire, a world of unrighteousness. The tongue is set among our members, staining the whole body, setting on fire the entire course of life, and set on fire by hell." The words we speak can be blessings or curses. I tell parents and guardians of children to speak positively to and about their children every day and to look for right behavior that can be rewarded over wrong behavior that can be reprimanded. For each one thing children do wrong, they do nine things worthy of praise. So the adults in their life should brag on them and tell them they're loved, valued, and talented every day.

The little saying "Sticks and stones may break my bones but words will never hurt me" could not be more false. Words do hurt. They can build up or tear down. That means our words have so much power in them that they should always inspire and lift others so they can see who they are in God's eyes. I wasn't accustomed to such positive language, and very few inspiring and uplifting conversations occurred in my home.

Bill ran a package store, and Mama worked long, hard hours doing all of the manual labor. By contrast, Bill was so lazy. He sat around the store or talked with customers while my mother unloaded the heavy boxes, restocked the shelves, and iced down the coolers. When she was finished for the day, she was exhausted, but when she came home, she made sure we were fed, bathed, and in bed.

Bill wouldn't get home until much later because he stayed out drinking after the store was closed. He was a heavy drinker, and our environment was filled with the fear of his abuse. He took out his violent anger on Mama the most, and he would stumble into the house drunk as could be and start an argument with her over the tiniest thing. Then he would beat her so badly that the police would come and arrest him. Even though I wasn't a Christian, I'd lie in bed anxiously praying, *God, please don't let Bill beat Mama tonight!* Even I knew just enough to call on Him when we had big trouble.

Some nights Bill went after me. One night when I was around nine, he came home drunk and heard some of our cows lowing out in the pasture. I heard him stumbling down the hallway toward my room as he hollered, "You little bastard, you didn't feed them cows enough hay when you got home from school. That's why they're making all that noise." Then he burst into my room and yelled, "Get up out of that bed and go feed those cows more hay right now!"

I was just a little boy, scared to death to go out to the dirty, old barn in the dark by myself. I wish I could say that was the only night something like that happened, but that was the normal way of life for me and my family. That's just the kind of man Bill was.

Throughout the seven years we spent with Bill, we probably left at least 20 times. Mama would come home in a panic and tell Rhonda and me to grab whatever we could and pack our clothes because we were leaving. Some nights she ran into our rooms while we were sleeping and shook us awake, saying, "Get up! We gotta get outta here before Bill gets home!" It took us less than five minutes to stuff our suitcases and get out of there.

Then we'd hide out somewhere because we knew Bill would be looking for us, calling everyone Mama knew. Then when he found out where we were, he'd show up to convince Mama to come back.

We did go back. We *always* went back.

Years later, when I was grown, my mother shared more about her experiences with Bill, things I'd never known. I'd seen the physical bruises, but I hadn't always realized her emotional heartache. She said before Bill began beating her, he would say things like, "I'm going to mess up your face so bad no other man will want to look at you." Hearing such terrible details broke my heart all over again.

I asked Mama why we went back so many times. She explained, "Benny, I had only a sixth-grade education, and I didn't have any way to provide for you and your sister. So I worked in the package store for Bill just to provide a roof over your heads and food on the table for y'all. I felt like I didn't have any other choice."

We were housed, fed, and clothed, but it wasn't a happy home, and the long-term effects of living with Bill followed me well into adulthood.

If anyone had grounds for explaining away bad behavior and poor decision-making, it was me. I could have easily chosen the wrong path in my late teens and early twenties and blamed every bad choice on my experiences with Bill. They could have become my go-to excuses for a wild, rebellious lifestyle.

Each day, people all across this country sit in counseling sessions explaining how their behaviors are simply a product of their upbringing. Parents who yelled at or hit them are the cause of their anger and self-control issues. Alcoholics in the home are to blame for their issues with substance abuse. Their broken homes are responsible for their infidelity. And strict, religious parents are the root cause of their rebellious tendencies.

People use these types of excuses themselves or allow other people to speak them into their lives. Whatever the case may be, they're stuck in these patterns of behavior and thinking because they can't get past the past. They've allowed themselves to become victims of their circumstances.

I'm certainly not discounting the lifelong effects traumatic experiences can have on an individual, but as someone who is all too familiar with childhood trauma, I am here to say you do not have to be defined by what happened to you. You do not have to live your life as a product of the environment you were raised in or the horrible experiences you endured in your past. You see, while you can't determine what happens *to* you, you can determine what happens *in* you. You alone decide how you respond to all situations.

God defied the odds in my life when, as a young adult, I let Him grow me beyond what I thought I could become. At first, I listed all the reasons He couldn't use me, but I was building walls and limiting the space where He wanted to work in my life. Not until I traded in my excuses for trust did God begin moving and working in ways I never thought possible. He used my past to create a path for my future.

God will begin defying the odds in your life when you refuse to let your circumstances become excuses and realize the power you have over your own thoughts and behaviors. Then He can begin a transformation in you that you could never have imagined.

In Romans 12:2, Paul advises Christians, "Do not be conformed to this world, but be transformed by the renewal of your mind, that by testing you may discern what is the will of God, what is good and acceptable and perfect." Letting your past experiences dictate your plans and potential is the perfect example of conforming to the patterns of this world. While you may create a resumé that disqualifies you from a variety of opportunities, renewing your mind with God's truth allows Him to use your experiences to create a resumé that qualifies you for His kingdom work.

Often, the greatest hurts, the hardest hits, and the most painful circumstances are what allow God to deliver the greatest blessings. I have often said that our strongest passions come out of our deepest hurts. God wants to work through your circumstances and use your experiences to grow you and develop your testimony. When you allow Him to take what the Enemy meant for evil and turn it into a blessing, He gets all the glory. Only then do you become a victor instead of a victim.

While my childhood experiences were often painful to remember, I knew healing would come only once I let God have every bit of the hurt. I also had to trust Him to use those painful experiences for my good and His glory. And not only did He bring healing to my broken heart but He created in me a passion for providing children with positive, encouraging, and Christian environments.

God chose to defy the odds against my healing through the vision of Rock Springs Christian Academy and the Rock Springs Recreational Complex. Today our original campus houses a private, Christian school and learning center that provides a godly educational environment for children beginning at six weeks of age. The children enrolled in our school receive a strong education built on the foundation of God's Word, and families in our area participate in community athletic programs at our recreational facility, led by godly individuals who encourage children in their talents and abilities.

If I had chosen to hold on to the hurt from my past, I would have missed out on the vision for the future of so many others in and around Rock Springs. I have never once regretted letting go of my hurt and trusting God to heal. He has always done more with my pain than I ever dreamed possible. He has always defied the odds.

God wants to do the very same thing in your life through your most painful circumstances. He wants to take the experience with abuse and use it to help others heal. He wants to take the hurt of a broken home and provide counseling for couples facing divorce. He wants to take the neglect from an alcoholic parent and use it to serve in a 12-step program. Whatever your hurt may be, God will use it to help others and further His kingdom.

He will not reach out and take the hurt from you, though. He's waiting for you to lay it all down at His feet and trust Him to do a mighty work. You must be willing to give it all to Him before He will use it for good.

I'm not foolish enough to think this is an easy task. I know from experience that it's incredibly difficult to let go of deep hurt and trust that healing will come. Therefore, I want to provide you with a few application points to help you take the necessary steps to move from victim to victor.

Realize the Responsibility You Have

Maintaining a victim mentality requires keeping a thought pattern that says you're helpless and incapable of changing your circumstances. But if you want to see God defy the odds in your life through your hurt, you must realize the responsibility you have over the choices you make each day.

You don't have to live your life believing you're weak or incapable of overcoming your past. Freedom from all sin and hurt can be found in Jesus, but it's up to you to receive it. First John 4:4 says, "He who is in you is greater than he who is in the world." That means you do not have to allow the circumstances of this life to overwhelm or limit you. The choice is yours to pursue a future not determined by your past. And with the Holy Spirit living inside of you, the power to overcome any obstacle is already present.

Choosing to believe there is purpose in your pain is incredibly difficult; it's so easy to question why God would allow such terrible things to happen to you. But you will never move to a place of permanent healing unless you choose to believe that better days lie ahead. You must choose to deny your feelings and trust the Father every day. You must choose to believe that affliction builds character and prepares you for a greater purpose. Every inch of your worldly heart will tell you that your circumstances define who you are, but you must daily choose to believe that you are not defined by your circumstances but by how you respond to them.

You must first realize the incredible power that lies within the choices you make. I'm not talking about the major life choices that come over the course of your life but the small choices you make every day. Never underestimate the power of small choices, because small choices lead to great choices. It may be a trial by the mile, but it's a cinch by the inch. Overcoming life's greatest hurts doesn't happen overnight, but little by little you can choose to allow your greatest tragedies to build your best testimony.

Choosing to move past your circumstances into a place of healing can be the most difficult step. Yet you're the only one who can choose to move forward without your past hurts dictating your life. You are in control of your own thoughts and actions. You are the one responsible for deciding how your past impacts your future.

Give Your Hurt to God

Whether you've suffered through terrible experiences in your past or you're currently enduring a difficult situation, you can have victory through relying completely on God. Beginning to move forward is a huge step that should be celebrated, but you must not stop there. Making better choices is just the first step in your healing. To truly witness God defying the odds in your life, you must give your hurt to Him, the healer.

God is capable of bringing healing to any heart no matter how severe the trauma. No heart is so shattered that He can't bring restoration. Anything placed in His hand—no matter the damage—can be made better. But if you don't surrender your hurt to God, it will remain a memory and won't become a ministry. God has a purpose for every heartache you experience, and surrendering everything to Him paves the way for kingdom work.

When you give your hurt to God, you can exchange it for His truth. You can exchange bitterness for forgiveness. You can replace the lies of the Enemy with the truth of your Savior. Matthew 11:28 shows God's heart for those who are hurting. Jesus said, "Come to me, all who labor and are heavy laden, and I will give you rest." God wants you to take everything to Him because He cares for you and wants you to experience the peace only He can provide.

Giving your past to God allows you to receive more than you ever lost. While He restores what was broken through your healing, He also brings redemption by making your circumstances better than they were. God will always give you more when you trust Him with your hurt.

Let God Use Your Hurt

God has allowed painful circumstances in your life for a reason: He wants to use all you have experienced to grow your faith and impact others for eternity. Do not despise what you have experienced or what you're currently going through, because God has great plans to use every hurt to bring people to Himself. He wants to use your testimony to help others walk through their darkest times.

In Mark 5, Jesus heals a man who is possessed with a demon. The man pleads to go with Him, but Jesus doesn't allow him to do that. In verse 19, He tells the man, "Go home to your friends and tell them how much the Lord has done for you, and how he has had mercy on you." Being with Jesus was the man's only focus, but Jesus knew his testimony would cause others to believe, that it would change the lives of those around him.

The same is true for your testimony. Let God use it to impact those around you for eternity. When people know you have overcome circumstances similar to their own, they connect with you and grow more willing to let you closer to their hurt. In that place of empathy, then, you can point them to Christ, and they can begin healing as well. God wants to use you. He wants you to be His hands and feet to lead others and be His voice of encouragement that offers hope in dark times. He will create a ministry out of your misery. He will give purpose to your pain.

The author of Psalm 119:71 says, "It is good for me that I was afflicted, that I might learn your statutes." Affliction brings us closer to God and strengthens our faith. Let God have your past, and you will learn all that He has planned for your future.

God will defy the odds in your life when you allow Him to move you from a victim to a victor. And you must *allow* Him to move; He will not force you to let go of your hurt in order to experience healing. While it may be the most difficult step to take, you can overcome any hardship when you realize the power of your choices, let God have your hurt, and trust Him to purpose your pain for His kingdom.

Don't let your hurt keep you in bondage. God has so much more for your life—the life of a victor!

2

THE COMPANY
YOU KEEP

O ver the years I've learned that God often works in the most unlikely and unusual ways, but He moves using methods that require that all glory be given to Him alone. That's exactly what happened in my life when I was 12 years old.

I mentioned earlier that, until I was 30, I believed my biological father was Lee Tate, whom my mother had married when I was very young. He was a veteran and a coal miner who lived in Palmer, Tennessee, and he legally adopted Rhonda and me, signed our birth certificates, and gave us the name Tate even though he wasn't the biological father to either of us. I thought he died when I was very young.

Well, even though I never knew him, Lee made a huge impact on my life.

When the fire in their hasty relationship burned out, Lee and my mother never actually filed paperwork to finalize their divorce. Odd, yes, but God loves to move and work in the oddest of circumstances. Lee actually died when I was in seventh grade, and because he and my mother were still married, she was able to draw his Social Security check, his veteran's check, and his black lung benefit for his years as a coal miner.

When the details of this unusual situation all fell into place, Mama once again told us to pack our things in a hurry. This time was different, she said. We were leaving Bill for good. She now had income of her own and could provide for Rhonda and me without relying on him.

God had made a way for us to get out from under the control and abuse we had endured for seven years. And He promises He will always make a way through every difficult circumstance. In Isaiah 43:19, God said, "Behold, I am doing a new thing; now it springs forth, do you not perceive it? I will make a way in the wilderness and rivers in the desert." Living with Bill was certainly a dry wasteland, but God had a plan that would defy the odds in our lives in such a way that only He could receive the glory.

We packed everything we could fit into our suitcases and fled. It was never easy to find a place to stay whenever we left Bill because he would always come looking for us—and with the threat of murder. One time he said he would hunt us down if we ever left again, come through the front door with a gun, and shoot until everyone was dead. You can imagine why people weren't exactly volunteering to take us in when we were on the run from a man like that.

This time Mama turned to a friend named Clydia Northcutt, nicknamed Ram. She lived about an hour away and had agreed to take us in for two or three weeks. I've always felt gratitude toward Clydia for helping us when the risk was so high. But now I realize that a woman doesn't get nicknamed Ram for no reason—she wasn't a lady you wanted to pull a gun on because she would probably aim one twice as big right back at you! Ram was no stranger to a lifestyle like ours, one that included a rough-around-the-edges kind of people and dangerous situations. She knew exactly what she was getting into, and she got into it anyway.

Throughout the years, I have often stopped in to see Clydia and again express my appreciation for what she did for my family so many years ago. I encourage you to always take the time to express gratitude to those who have helped you along the way. As I've said, God often positions people in our lives at just the right time to be an influence on us in the direction we should go. Clydia was certainly that kind of influence. Mama said we had left for good, and she meant it, but without Clydia, we could've ended up back with Bill—or worse, dead.

A Timely Rescue

Now that my mother had a steady income of her own, we were able to rent a single-wide trailer in Altamont, Tennessee, a little town high on top of the mountain. It certainly wasn't home sweet home; the trailer was so small. But we didn't have many belongings to fill it anyway. Besides, it was hard to settle into a place when we might have to up and leave at any moment. We constantly lived in fear of Bill finding us and keeping his promise to kill us.

We knew he'd again been calling people Mama knew to determine our whereabouts. They would claim to know nothing and then call Mama, warning, "Bill is still looking for you. He says when he finds you, he's going to kill all three of you." Each night, Mama, Rhonda, and I all climbed into the same bed to sleep because we were so afraid Bill would show up in the middle of the night.

And that's just what happened.

It was well after midnight when headlights flashed through our windows and a car pulled up. I looked out to see a red Cadillac parked right at our front steps. Bill got out of that car, then stomped up to the porch and began beating on the front door so hard I was sure it would burst open. He cursed and hollered threats of death with each pounding of his fist. We were terrified; we just knew he was going to break down the door and kill us.

As I watched from the window, he finally quit beating on the door and walked back to his car. I remember thinking, *Maybe he's leaving. Maybe he's really leaving.* Deep down, though, I knew better. He climbed into the car and began backing out, positioning the Cadillac as if he were about to pull out of the driveway. But that's not what he did. He reached into his glove compartment and grabbed a gun before putting it into his jacket pocket. Then he got out of the car, left it running with the driver's side door open, and returned to the front porch.

While this was happening, Mama yelled, "Rhonda, call the law!

Call nine-one-one!" Now as Rhonda dialed, Bill began kicking the front door as if to tear it from the hinges. We were sure it was over for us.

Then just as he was about to kick in the door, no more than a minute or so after Rhonda had called for help, we heard a siren and saw a police car stop right in front of our driveway. A deputy sheriff named Joe Sons jumped out of his car and ran across our yard. As he leaped onto our front porch, Bill reached into his pocket, and Joe said, "Sir, if you go for that gun, it will be the worst mistake you will ever make."

Bill insisted he wasn't doing anything wrong, that he was only at our house to talk to my mother. But Joe said, "It's no hour to be talking to anybody." Then he cuffed Bill right there on the porch and placed him in the back of his police car.

Before leaving, Joe came into our house to make sure we were safe and hadn't been hurt. Mama thanked him, then said, "The sheriff's office is at least five or ten minutes away. How did you get here so fast?"

"Well," Joe said, "when I got the call, I just happened to be patrolling right in front of your trailer."

Officer Sons may have believed that just happened, but I know God placed him there at just the right time.

Bill went to jail that night but was released the next morning. Officer Sons drove him back to our trailer to get his car, and as Bill got into his Cadillac to leave, Joe warned, "Listen, I'm going to follow you off this mountain, and you better never come back. If you ever bother this woman and her two children again, it will be a sad day for you. It will be the worst decision you'll ever make."

Just as God had positioned Jenny Travis and Clydia Northcutt in our lives at the right moment, He used Deputy Sheriff Joe Sons to end our toxic and violent connection with Bill. And that truly was the end of our story with this abusive man. We never heard from him again, and we no longer lived in fear for our lives.

As the circumstances began to change in my life, I was certain the odds would begin to shift in my favor. But that wasn't exactly the case. We may have been free from Bill, but plenty of obstacles lay ahead.

Life in Altamont

Mama, Rhonda, and I had been given a fresh start in Altamont, one of those little towns in the hills where folks still believed the earth was flat, wrestlin' was real, and nobody had ever walked on the moon. But we were no longer living in a constant state of fear, and Mama had a steady income to provide for our family. Don't misunderstand me; we were still poor. But everyone in our little town was poor, so we didn't actually know just how poor we were. We had enough to eat and pay the few bills we owed each month.

Altamont was full of hard-working mountain folks, made up of family-owned small businesses that barely made ends meet, a beer joint, single-wide trailers like ours, hound dogs, and old pickup trucks—the kinds of things that make up a good country song. (The two songs everyone knew were "Rocky Top" and "The Star-Spangled Banner"—in that order.) We all lived day-to-day and paycheck-to-paycheck. Some made their money on the up-and-up while others were on the wrong side of the law. But we had enough money to make Altamont our home as we made a fresh start in life. I was hopeful about what the future would bring.

We were free to move on with our lives and establish healthy, stable roots in our new community. However, not everyone adjusts to new-found freedom the way they should; freedom can be an overwhelming temptation for those who've been trapped in a controlling situation for a very long time. Now free from Bill, Mama was able to go wherever she pleased, become friends with whomever she chose, and make decisions she'd not been allowed to make for herself in our previous situation.

So instead of establishing healthy, stable roots, our home had become a different unstable environment with no stable parental influence to nurture and direct Rhonda and me. We had no real structure or support, and it just wasn't a responsible time in my mother's life.

My sister and I were also four years apart in age, which meant we were at different stages in our lives, and we didn't have a very close relationship. Working hard to finish high school so she could enroll in community college to become a draftsman, Rhonda had plans for her future and was stepping out on her own. So between Mama's life and my sister's, I was pretty much alone at age 12. I often stayed with our neighbors. They were a caring couple who lived in a little shotgun house, and I would sleep on their couch night after night until Mama pulled into the front yard and honked the horn.

My early teen years would best be described as a very lonely time. I didn't have anyone to check in on my whereabouts, keep up with my academic progress, or take any interest in my life. People who did show up in my home certainly weren't examples of responsibility or moral conduct. I was on my own with no boundaries. So whenever I wasn't spending my free time alone, I was hanging out with the wrong crowd. I didn't have much choice in who my friends were because any respectable, caring parent in the area made sure their child didn't hang out with a boy from the wrong side of the tracks. My family's reputation limited me to friends who also had absent parents and a dysfunctional home life.

Concerning how to raise children, Ephesians 6:4 tell parents to "bring them up in the discipline and instruction of the Lord." Proper discipline and instruction can be the greatest showing of love to a child. Children crave both because they show they are loved and cared for by their parents or guardians. But I had no one pointing me in the right direction whatsoever during this time of my life.

In Deuteronomy 6:6-7, God said, "These words that I command you today shall be on your heart. You shall teach them diligently to your children, and shall talk of them when you sit in your house, and when you walk by the way, and when you lie down, and when you rise." But there was no one in my home sharing positive life lessons with me much less biblical truths either. There wasn't even a parental figure to talk to at home—or anywhere.

I used to wonder what it would be like to have a father put his arm around my shoulders and give me a few pointers after football practice. I wondered what it would be like to sit around a dinner table as a family in the evening, with each person sharing stories about their day. I certainly didn't know what any of that was like, and the odds of me making the right choices during this time and years to come were growing slimmer.

During my eighth-grade year, we bought a little house in Altamont. It was a small cinder-block building with no insulation and wood-burning stoves at both ends to heat the place—not the picture-perfect family home by any means. Then not long after we moved in, we began illegally selling whiskey out the back door. Our county was considered a dry county, so we had to drive about an hour to Manchester, Tennessee, to buy the alcohol. With the car loaded down, we would haul it back to our house and sell it during all hours of the night.

I no longer lived in fear of suffering abuse, but I did fear the police pulling us over on the drive home and seeing our car loaded down with alcohol. They would most certainly know what we were up to, and I was sure they would haul us to jail. But just like all of the other dysfunctional things in my life, this lifestyle became a new normal, and those trips became less and less worrisome. When you've lived a certain way for most of your life, it can be hard to see that what you're doing is wrong. I really didn't know other kids were living a life much different from mine.

People would knock on the back door late at night, and Mama would holler, "Benny, get up and sell that whiskey!" One night when I opened the door about midnight, an arm came through and presented a badge. He wasn't a regular customer, but he was certainly interested in the whiskey we were selling. I hollered back to Mama, "I think this one is here to see you!" At this point, we had been selling so long that the sheriff knew about our operation, but the badge that came through the door that night was from no county officer. He was a state agent who had no intentions of turning a blind eye.

Just like that, our whiskey-selling operation was shut down. I would be lying if I said I wasn't relieved, but I didn't even have time to imagine living a shiny, new life before Mama told me the new plan. We would be moving out of our house and making it a nightclub where people could drink, carouse, and carry on with all types of wild and often illegal behavior.

We went from selling whiskey to running a nightclub as if the odds for success were any better in that line of work. I often talk about the "lounge lizards down at the Crystal Pistol" in my sermons, and our nightclub is the reason I know so much about those kinds of people. It was full of lounge lizards!

Soon I was maturing and trying to figure out who I was with little or no support from stable adults in my life. I enjoyed playing sports in school, but a parent never attended any of my games and cheer from the stands with the other moms and dads.

My school was about 20 miles from where I lived, and participating in sports meant I had to walk home from practice or try to catch a ride from someone. But I turned to playing football and baseball in the afternoons anyway to avoid going straight home after school. I wasn't the best athlete, but playing sports was the only thing that provided some type of structure.

I always describe my position on the football team as a *tailback*, because when I eagerly jumped up to go out on the field, my coach would always yell, "Boy, get your tail back on that bench!" The odds against my earning an athletic scholarship or any other athletic recognition were high, but that didn't get me down. At least I didn't have to go home to an empty house right after school, so I was perfectly happy being a *tailback* for the football team.

The influences in my life continued to get worse both at home and within my circle of friends. The majority of the people I knew were involved with either drugs, alcohol, or illegal activity. It came as no surprise to anyone that I quickly began to resemble those around me in both behavior and decision-making.

As a young teenager, I didn't realize how important the company I kept could be. To be honest, I didn't give much thought at all to the reputation of those around me. The criteria for hanging out with me included being poor and lacking parental guidance. If we had that in common, we were buddies. I never really thought about the long-term influence those friends would have on my life.

◆

I encourage you to carefully consider the company you keep. Regardless of your current stage of life, the people you habitually associate with will influence you in powerful ways. You must keep in mind that every person who enters your life will do one of two things: lift you up or pull you down. Therefore, you can't afford to move through life with anyone unless you first consider the potential impact they'll have on your future.

Proverbs 13:20 teaches, "Whoever walks with the wise becomes wise, but the companion of fools will suffer harm." Continuing this lesson, Proverbs 27:17 says, "Iron sharpens iron, and one man sharpens another." Both verses emphasize the importance of other people's influence over our lives. Therefore, we must take a closer look at those with whom we associate most frequently and acknowledge their impact.

Henry Ford was once asked who he considered his best friend. His response? "My best friend is the one who brings out the best in me."[1] Ford realized the important role his close friends and associates had on his success. If you want to see God defy the odds in your life, you must take a look at your circle of influence to see if you're being lifted up or pulled down. God probably won't move in mighty ways if your group isn't concerned with growth.

Making changes to the company you keep will always be an uncomfortable process. The people who pull you down won't understand the choices you make to bring positive change to your life. Often, those people will respond with criticism and condemnation. They may even attack your character and attempt to place doubt in your mind. Proverbs 12:15 explains this response: "The way of a fool is right in his own eyes." Those who are pulling you down don't see the negative impact their words and actions have on you, so the transition toward positive, uplifting relationships can be painful and often lonely.

A point came when I realized I had become like those I was associating with and had made a lot of the same mistakes my "friends" had. I knew a change had to take place, but I wasn't prepared for how difficult it would be. It was not an overnight process, and it left me enduring long periods of loneliness. But once I began associating with people who lifted me up, God was able to work in incredible ways because I was no longer allowing the negative influences of others to stand in His way.

If you think the people influencing your life are interfering with God's ability to grow you and use you, I'm here to tell you that changes are not only necessary but worth every uncomfortable step toward healthy associations. I learned so much from my own difficult experiences, and I want to offer a few practical steps to help you move in the direction of stronger, healthier relationships.

Create Two Circles

Making necessary changes to the company you keep does not mean cutting everyone who doesn't know Christ out of your life. Avoiding interactions with lost people is not what Christians are called to do. Cultivating healthy relationships and associations in your life doesn't mean division; it means distance. Instead of cutting people out, focus on implementing substantial boundaries. Creating two distinct circles for relationships can help put those boundaries in place to determine the amount of influence and impact others have on your life.

Circle One – Your Inner Circle

This group of people is known as your inner circle, and it should consist of close Christian friends and godly influences. That's because everyone in it should continually lift you up and point you toward Jesus. This is true whether you've been a Christian most of your life, have just recently experienced salvation, or have never accepted Jesus into your life, but the reason varies according to which category you're in.

Those of you who have been Christians for many years must have an inner circle of godly influences in order to maintain stamina in your walk with Christ. The author of Hebrews 12:1-2 wrote, "Let us run with endurance the race that is set before us, looking to Jesus, the founder and perfecter of our faith," and in James 5:11, James wrote, "Behold, we consider those blessed who remained steadfast." Living a life that glorifies God can be difficult and exhausting at times. Making the right choices day and in day out can be tough when the world tempts you to move in the opposite direction. Yet you are called to endure and be relentless in your pursuit of Christ. God will use your inner circle of godly influences to speak life into your weakest moments, to pray for you throughout difficult seasons of life, and to encourage you in making the right decisions.

Some of you may have recently experienced salvation and are beginning to see how quickly the world tries to pull you back into your old habits and relationships. Having an inner circle of godly influences will provide you with the wisdom and direction you need as you begin your walk with Christ. Strong Christian friends can help guide you in your Bible study, get you plugged into church organizations, and be a source of accountability when worldly temptations try to sabotage the positive changes you're making.

And then some of you may have never experienced salvation, to which I say that must be the first step you take before God can defy the odds in your life. He wants a relationship with you more than He wants to fix all of the areas you see as problematic. When you come to know Christ and pursue a personal relationship with Him, He begins transforming your life in ways you never thought possible. He doesn't simply change your circumstances; He changes your heart, and then you'll want to surround yourself with others who have experienced that heart change as well.

As you begin to create an inner circle of godly influences, God will begin working in your heart and draw you to Himself. He will use that inner circle to pray for you and point you to Jesus in every area of your life.

My inner circle consists of other pastors who point me to Jesus and small-group members who share life with my wife and me. All of the people in my inner circle want not what they think is best for me but what Jesus wants for me. They push me and stretch me in my pursuit of God. And many of them are way further along in their walk with Christ, which allows me to learn and grow from their wisdom and experience. I know with certainty that my inner circle is praying for me daily as I am praying daily for them. I truly believe trying to live life without a distinct inner circle only makes the journey all the more difficult.

Circle Two–Your Outer Circle

This group is known as your outer circle and should consist of the people in your life who may not have a relationship with Jesus and who do not consistently lift you up. Many times these people are old friends, coworkers, or even family members you have to see on a regular basis. But while they may play consistent roles in your life, they can do so at a healthy distance.

Old friends and coworkers may be the easiest people to distance yourself from when creating your outer circle. It's natural for friendships to evolve over time and for coworkers to have distinct boundaries when it comes to personal relationships. You can continue to support old friends and coworkers through various seasons of life and serve as a source of prayer and encouragement for them, but you may have to say no to invitations to participate in activities you no longer view as acceptable for you and to minimize your shared time and spaces.

Family members can often be the hardest to distance yourself from when creating an outer circle. Everyone has relatives they love and care for who are not sources of encouragement or godly influences. Creating distance between yourself and such family members can seem harsh, and your loved ones may direct critical, negative comments your way. Most often, they will at least not understand the choices you're making for your life.

While choosing to place certain people in your outer circle and then creating necessary distance can be a daunting task, it doesn't have to be motivated by anything other than love and respect. You are showing love and respect for yourself as you set important boundaries, which in turn allows you to better position yourself to be a positive influence in the lives of others.

I have learned the benefit of creating two distinct circles in my life when it comes to relationships. Yet creating them is the easiest part of the process. The challenge is in maintaining them. Once you have set clear boundaries for each of your circles, you must be diligent in keeping the necessary distance from your outer circle while also keeping consistent, positive influence in your inner circle. While this continual process is indeed challenging, it can be made easier through better decision-making skills and new habits.

Create New Habits

Businessman Charles "Tremendous" Jones believed that the people you associate with and the books you read determine where you will be in five years.[2] This belief greatly impacted my life as a young adult, because I realized how important my daily decisions would be for my future success. While I may have the right people in proximity to my life, I must also create habits that propel me forward rather than hold me back.

Be a Reader

Mr. Jones's belief encouraged me to create the habit of reading one book every week. While many people never or rarely read a book, I encourage you to make reading a habit. Leaders are readers. Whether leading in the workplace or in the home, reading will help you continually develop new skills and gain new perspectives. You are meant to be a lifelong learner.

Also, carefully consider all content you're consuming—whatever the source—and evaluate how much it is challenging and growing you.

Be a Mentor and a Mentee

Placing an importance on mentorship is another great habit to create in your life. God provides a perfect example of mentorship in the book of Acts as well as in Paul's letters to Timothy. I believe mentorship is a vital habit, which is why I encourage you to always have a Paul and Timothy in your life.

A Paul should be someone who is older and wiser than you and further along in their walk with Christ. In fact, you may have more than one Paul because no one person is qualified to mentor you in every area of life. Your spiritual mentor will most likely be different from your financial mentor. Find people who are where you want to be and get your pail to their well!

A Timothy should be someone who is not as far along as you are in certain areas, including perhaps their walk with Christ. You will serve as a mentor to them as you pour into their lives with experience, knowledge, and spiritual guidance. Having them in your life is a necessary habit, because it will require continual growth on your part, developing dependence on the Holy Spirit to guide you in what wisdom you should share.

Creating circles of influence and creating new habits that ensure your continual growth are vitally important to seeing God defy the odds in your life. Growth is hard work, but God rewards hard work. You should pray as if everything depends on Him and work as if everything depends on you—especially concerning habits that strengthen you in your daily walk and prepare you for His plans. The impact of your relationships and your daily habits is far too significant in determining your future success to let either continue without careful consideration.

So be careful about the company you keep and embrace. You won't regret it.

3

COMMIT TO A TOTAL TURNAROUND

As I've more than hinted, an honest description of my life as an early teen would include skirting around the law, going wherever I wanted, staying with whomever I liked, and following the wrong crowds. My family was dysfunctional, resources were non-existent, I had very little athletic ability, and my grades were terrible. In addition, I earned a good paddling quite a few times at school.

No one thought I was on the road to a successful future, and I certainly didn't have any big hopes and dreams for myself. I'm so glad the plans and expectations we have for our lives pale in comparison to all God has in store for us.

My eighth-grade graduation was a milestone. First, for once Mama attended a school function. She sat in that tiny auditorium filled with wooden theater seats to watch me and 22 other eighth graders graduate. I wore a hand-me-down checkered suit we borrowed from a family friend, and I wasn't being honored for any major achievements, but nothing could have made me feel more special than seeing my mom attend the ceremony. Sure, I was happy to complete eighth grade, but her support meant more than any certificate.

Second, once again, God moved uniquely at just the right time—He used our principal, Phyllis Lusk, to speak into my life. She had been the one to paddle my backside many times, but God also used her voice to speak into my future. As the short ceremony came to an end, Mrs. Lusk gave a final speech to all the graduates. She talked about how proud she was of us and how she knew our futures were bright.

Then she said, "I look out across this auditorium and I see doctors. I see lawyers. I see teachers. I see firemen. I even see a preacher." And at that very moment, the Lord said to me, *It's you.*

Now, I didn't know the Lord, and we didn't go to church, but God used Mrs. Lusk to place a calling in my heart. I didn't know exactly what I was feeling, but it made my heart beat a little faster, and I could have sworn Mrs. Lusk was looking right at me when she said, "I even see a preacher." For a moment, her words made me consider what my future could possibly hold.

I wish I could say my life changed that day, that I immediately got saved and lived a better life. But that wasn't the way my story played out. While that day was momentous for me, reality hit as soon as we walked out the doors of that little auditorium and went back to running a nightclub and hanging with all the wrong crowds.

Around this same time, Mama started seeing a man who ran an amusement business. I've always been pretty sure he had some influence in her deciding to turn our old house into a nightclub. After all, he handled everything from gambling machines to pool tables. But as their relationship got serious, I got busy hanging out with my friends and running around town.

I had two good friends then. They were adopted twins, and they lived down the road from the beer joint where we shot pool together. I was a pretty good pool player, and the old guy at the beer joint (Friday was his name) would bet on me to win against other men. I didn't realize he was using me as a pawn to make money; I was in it for the free pool and soda. I also didn't mind people at the beer joint bragging on me, because it wasn't every day that compliments and encouragement came my way. I saw the whole situation as a win-win.

These two friends and I would hang out at the beer joint for a few hours a couple of days a week before heading back to their house to play basketball in their yard. They had a hard spot of dirt right next to the house where they'd hung an old, tattered basketball goal. We would dangle a lamp out the window of the house just so we could play a little longer after the sun went down.

You could have combined everything our two families had, and we still would have been dirt poor. But we didn't have a clue. And these boys were more like brothers to me than just friends. When we weren't playing basketball or pool, the three of us ran around together smoking, sneaking whiskey, and getting into trouble. Most of the time, though, we were just three boys figuring out how to waste time and do the silliest things we could think up.

Years later, as an adult, I learned the three of us had a lot more in common than just being three poor kids growing up in Altamont.

My biological father—still unknown to me—had a hand in these brothers being placed with their adoptive parents. His friend had gotten a young girl pregnant, but she couldn't raise the baby by herself and the guy wasn't sticking around to help her. My father had a way to help, though. After all, he knew a thing or two about shirking parental responsibility.

He knew a couple who couldn't have children, and if the girl would give birth, they would adopt her baby and give it a good home. She agreed to the plan and went through with the pregnancy, but to everyone's surprise, she delivered twins. The couple was happy to adopt both babies, and that's how my friends came to live in Altamont. The only thing my biological father gave me as I was growing up— unintentionally, might I add—was my two best friends. I guess they're the one thing I can thank him for giving me as a kid.

A string of random events—that's how I would have described my life up until I was 16 years old. I was simply living life as I pleased with no real boundaries or consequences to the poor decisions I was making. Nor did my future seem to extend beyond the county lines. If I ever dared to dream beyond the mountain, I always saw the odds stacked against me high, saying, *Yeah, right, boy*. After all, I was the kid from the wrong side of the tracks, and I had no business hoping for anything better. I had no talents or abilities, and even if I had any, I certainly didn't have the confidence to do anything with them.

Yet when God has placed a calling on your life, you can live away from Him on your own path for only so long. Proverbs 16:9 says, "The heart of man plans his way, but the LORD establishes his steps." I had my plans or lack thereof, but God had already determined my steps long before I was born. And I guess He decided that 16 years was long enough for me to be going down the wrong path, because that's when my life began to drastically change.

Mama's Surrender

Having moved out of the house we were running as a nightclub, we were renting a little place in Hubbards Cove, Tennessee, a small community at the foot of Altamont's mountain. Mama was also dating the man I mentioned before, and their relationship had become pretty serious.

Things seemed normal until I came home one day to find Mama in bed. I immediately knew something was wrong, because she was always an active woman. Her hair wasn't the only thing fiery; she had the personality to match. She was always on the go, never one to just sit around the house or sleep late.

Come to find out, Mama had learned that the man she was dating had been unfaithful to her for quite some time. She lay in bed all day, and when I would come home from school and check in on her, she'd respond, "Go away, Benny. Your mama's gonna be fine." In reality, my mother wasn't fine. She was battling depression and losing. Worse, Mama had decided she was too tired and hurt to keep going, and she'd decided to end her life.

Mama got up one morning and drove her red Thunderbird 30 miles to her first cousin Shirley's house in Manchester, the town where we bought the alcohol we sold illegally. She didn't want me to come home and find her dead body, so she thought she should end her life somewhere else.

Now, Shirley had caroused and lived a similar lifestyle to my mother's for many years. So it was a surprise when Mama arrived at Shirley's house, asking if she could "visit for a few days," and Shirley said, "Yes, you can, but I want you to know that Bill and I aren't the same people we used to be. We've gone down to Temple Baptist Church and given our lives to Christ. Bill and I are Christians, and more than anything, you need the Lord."

Shirley and her husband asked Mama if they could call their pastor to come talk to her. Mama agreed, admitting she was at her wits' end. He came that day and led my mother to the Lord. I've often said the very place Mama went to end her life is the place where she found life.

Early the next morning, Mama pulled into our driveway in her red Thunderbird. People may not believe me when I say this, but she looked different. She had a glow about her. She walked into the house and said, "Benny, your mama got saved last night! I haven't raised you right. We shouldn't have lived the way we've lived. And you shouldn't have lived the way I've let you live, boy. Your mama's sorry about that, but I want you to know you've got a new mama. I'm a different person."

I knew beyond a shadow of a doubt that my mother had been changed. The contrast between her old life and her new life as a saved woman was immediately evident. Hers had been a Damascus Road experience, and she *was* a different person! She went from a life of drinking, carousing, selling whiskey, and running a nightclub to giving it all up and going to church. I was amazed at her transformation and a little worried about what that meant for our lives. We had never lived any different, and I had no idea what this new life would look like.

Then Mama got a job at a little convenience store. After working there just a few days, she asked me to go with her down to the store to return the keys to the owner because she wouldn't be working there anymore. I asked her why she was quitting a job she'd just started, and she said, "They sell alcohol there. I've done enough damage through alcohol. I don't want to be responsible for others drinking any longer. I did enough to help people get alcohol while I was lost, and I sure don't want to be a part of it now that I'm a Christian." Mama was absolutely different.

She started going to church, and she also began praying for me. I know God heard her prayers, but the biggest impact on me was seeing the change in her. In Matthew 5:16, Jesus said, "In the same way, let your good deeds shine out for all to see, so that everyone will praise your heavenly Father" (NLT). I saw Mama's actions more than I heard her words.

Here I was 16 years old, and I had never been to church or heard my mother pray. After Mama got saved, at night I would go to my room to sleep and hear her in the next room praying out loud. She didn't know anything about the Bible. She wasn't praying Scripture or claiming the blessings and promises of God. She would simply pray, "God, I want Benny to get saved. I don't want my boy to go to hell. I know he's doing things he shouldn't be doing. Please don't let my boy go to hell!"

She knew I'd been doing things I had no business doing. And at this point, many of the friends I was running around with were starting to get into drugs. It wasn't just occasionally smoking pot here or there; they'd started experimenting with stronger drugs. To this day, many of the guys I ran around with then have never been able to get away from drugs. I've often thought about how pivotal this point was in my life. I could have gone in any direction.

My Salvation

I'm so glad Mama prayed. As I laid in my bed night after night, hearing her pray, God dealt with my heart. I would be out with my friends just hours earlier partying and seeming to have the time of my life, but when I came home and laid my head on the pillow, I was miserable. Something was missing in my heart. But I didn't understand that God had put eternity there (Ecclesiastes 3:11). I didn't know I was so miserable because *He* was what was missing. This went on for months and months—Mama constantly praying for me and me constantly miserable.

Clayton Jones was a preacher in our area who even before Mama got saved came by the house from time to time to invite us to his church. Rhonda had been going there for a while, and he knew the kind of people we were and the lifestyle we lived. Clayton had everything to lose and nothing to gain from associating with us in any way, but he genuinely cared. His love for people was more important to him than what others thought about him.

I always encourage people to invite others to church because they never know what God can do in a person's life. If we're faithful to extend the invitation, God will do the rest. To this day, I appreciate Clayton for never giving up on our family.

After Mama got saved, she would go hear Clayton preach and drag me along. I saw people getting saved during the services and told Clayton, "If I ever decide to do that, I certainly won't cry and carry on like those people did." He would just laugh and say, "Okay." Clayton had a way of loving people right where they were instead of trying to force salvation on them. He knew God was working in my heart, and he trusted His timing.

It happened one night, about midnight. I woke Mama up and told her I was so miserable that I just couldn't stand it anymore. She said, "Benny, you need the Lord." I was hesitant because it was so late, but Mama called Clayton, and he showed up in a suit and tie with his hair perfectly combed, looking fit for Sunday service.

I talked about how I was feeling, and he told me I needed to pray. Romans 10:13 says, "Everyone who calls on the name of the Lord will be saved." But I told him I didn't know how to pray. He grabbed hold of my hands, and we knelt in front of the couch there in my living room. I still believe everyone needs to pray.

I'll never forget every word he said as he led me in the sinner's prayer. He said, "Benny, it's as easy as A, B, C. Repeat after me: *Lord, I acknowledge I am a sinner. I believe You died on the cross for me. I confess my sin to You. Thank You for forgiving me. Thank You for saving me.*" It was a simple prayer, but it's not the length of the prayer; it's the strength of the prayer. Even now when I preach, I always lead people through the sinner's prayer in an elementary way because I envision a "Benny" out there who knows nothing about the church or God or prayer.

As Clayton led me through that prayer in the living room of our little house, tears streamed down my face and fell to the carpet. Then I told him I felt like a load had been lifted off my shoulders. He said, "I'm glad you feel that way, but God is not a feeling; He's a fact. No matter how you feel, Benny, you're saved because you've done what God's Word says to do."

Clayton stayed for a few hours just talking with us, and when I finally went to bed around 3:00 a.m., I had peace and joy like I'd never felt. I no longer had to worry about going to hell. You see, no one knew it, but I had been crying myself to sleep at night worried that I would die and go there. I was so happy that I could finally rest because I had accepted the Lord.

I didn't understand it then, but with my head on the pillow for just a short time, the Enemy attacked. I thought, *What am I going to tell my friends?* What in the world would I tell all the people I had been running around with, drinking and partying? I decided I would be a Christian but not tell anyone. I would be the same as I was before that night. I just didn't have to worry about going to hell.

I got only a few hours of sleep before waking up early the next morning. I got on my motorcycle, a Honda 350 four-cylinder street bike, and began riding those backroads around the valley just as the sun was coming up. It was such a peaceful ride. I saw things differently. I no longer saw just the sunrise, the trees, the animals; I saw what God had created. Things just had a different meaning now that I had accepted Christ.

A little way into my drive, I decided to stop at Franklin Johnson's service station. As I walked through the front door, there stood my good buddies, Tim and Frank—boys I had run around with doing all kinds of things I shouldn't have been doing. I had absolutely no intention of revealing what had happened the previous night, but I will never forget this if I live to be a hundred. I walked straight up to my friends and said, "Boys, the greatest thing happened to me last night. I got saved! I gave my life to the Lord."

I guess I just couldn't help myself.

Contagious Change

It started with those two boys, but for 40 years now, I've been telling people what Jesus did for me. I have never gotten over what He's done in the life of my family, and the difference God made reminds me of a story.

A man was testifying in front of a crowd at an old Salvation Army open-air meeting. He was telling everyone what the Lord had done for him when a heckler stood and yelled, "Sit down and shut up! You're dreaming!" As the heckler returned to his seat, a little girl tugged on his coat sleeve. She said, "That man who testified is my daddy. He used to drink all the time and come home and beat my mama. We didn't used to have any money, but now I have pretty dresses like this to wear. Now my daddy is so good to my mama. She smiles all the time, even when she's ironing. So if my daddy is dreaming, please, sir, don't wake him up!"

That would be the contrast in our family—in Mama's life and mine. God used my mother's salvation experience to change both our lives. She committed to a total turnaround after experiencing Jesus, and God used the example she set to impact my life just in the nick of time. To this day, most of the people I associated with during my teenage years are either battling addiction, serving a prison sentence, or dead. I was heading down the same road when my mother turned her life around and began praying for God to change my direction too.

After deciding to follow Christ, we never looked back. Everything about our lives had to change in order to follow Jesus—our associations, attitudes, thoughts, words, behaviors, and daily routines. I didn't have an extensive vocabulary to begin with, but I had to give up half of it when I got saved. No part of my old life could carry over into my new walk with Christ.

Our relationships with other family members began to change as well. What God had done caused many of them to become curious enough to hear our testimony and even accept our invitations to church. My grandmother, who'd lived a hard life and didn't know the Lord, accepted our invitation to attend a revival. After the first night, she was adamant that she would never go back. She said, "That preacher stared at me the entire time he spoke!" I knew what she felt was the Lord dealing with her heart, so Mama and I were relentless in inviting her to go for just one more service.

Granny came back a second night, and God dealt with her heart the whole service. When the altar call was made, the preacher looked right at her and said, "Why don't you come and pray." My grandmother gave her life to Christ that night as the preacher led her in the sinner's prayer and Mama knelt beside her. When she finished praying, she turned to my mother and said, "Melba, I love you."

A few weeks later, Mama gave her testimony in front of the church during an evening service. She proudly told the congregation, "My mother gave her life to Christ, and that same night she told me she loved me for the first time in my entire life."

When Christ came into Granny's heart, she experienced love like never before. First John 3:14 says, "We know that we have passed out of death into life, because we love the brothers. Whoever does not love abides in death." God is love; therefore, when He comes into your heart and life, you're never the same. A person who experiences the love of Christ can't help but love others.

God began defying the odds against my family when Mama and I surrendered every area of our lives to Him. We certainly weren't perfect, and we failed to get it right many times, but the attitude of our hearts was to please God. Seeing God defy the odds in every area of your life requires you to get off the fence and become recognizable as Christ's follower—daily. While there's no such thing as a perfect Christian, you can commit each day to striving for holiness.

Get Off the Fence

Committing to a total turnaround requires you to clearly choose a side of the fence—the new side of your future, not the old side of your past. Choosing to remain on the fence paralyzes you because it keeps you from moving in any direction. The uncertainty in your life will remain as long as you straddle the fence.

Here's the catcher: God won't provide perfect peace in your circumstances unless you give them completely to Him. There is no peace outside of God; therefore, you can't keep one foot in His ways and the other foot in worldly ways. That leaves you with feet heading in opposite directions! First John 2:15 says, "Do not love the world or the things in the world. If anyone loves the world, the love of the Father is not in him." You must make a clear choice concerning which side of the fence you're on.

In Deuteronomy 30:15-16, God is clear about the choices we're given each day:

> See, I set before you today life and good, death and evil. If you obey the commandments of the LORD your God that I command you today, by loving the LORD your God, by walking in his ways, and by keeping his commandments and his statutes and his rules, then you shall live and multiply, and the LORD your God will bless you in the land that you are entering to take possession of it.

In many seasons of life, I've been on the verge of entering new "land" I wanted to possess—salvation, Bible college, preaching, marriage, parenting, and so much more. Because I wanted His blessing over my life, each time I had to make up my mind that I would love God above all else, walk in obedience even when it was uncomfortable, and keep His commands over what the world said was popular.

God wants to bless your life greatly. He wants to increase all that you have and lead you in a life that is abundantly more than you could ever imagine for yourself. But with each promise of blessing is a requirement: You must commit fully to the Lord and His ways. You will never fulfill God's purpose for your life with one foot in and one foot out. In order to see the life, prosperity, and blessing God promises, you have to commit to getting off the fence and moving toward Him.

You may be in a season right now when you're on the verge of entering a "land" you wish to possess. Maybe it's a new job or a new business venture. Or you're on the verge of marriage or entering a new relationship. Some of you may be entering the land of parenthood. Whatever new land you find yourself entering, you certainly aren't hoping for failure; you're hoping for success. I'm sure you're preparing ahead to make sure things go as smoothly as possible, like weighing all options for business opportunities, discussing relationship values and goals with your significant other, or child proofing every area of your home.

But while preparing ahead in such ways is incredibly important, the most significant preparation you can make is deciding to give those areas over to God—completely. You can't keep parts of your business for yourself while letting God have only the parts that are struggling. You can't navigate the highs of the relationship on your own and seek God's presence only when you find your relationship in the valley. You can't expect God to remain on the back burner while you raise a healthy child only to call on Him when sickness or injury comes. God wants every area of your life, the highs and the lows.

When you give everything over to God, then all areas of the business, all stages of the relationship, and all fearful moments with your child will far exceed your expectations. The highs will be so much higher, but the lows won't seem quite so low. God will move in every area, providing peace as He delivers on His promise of life and prosperity. A clear choice has to be made, and it requires you to get off the fence.

Become Recognizable

Choosing a side of the fence is just the beginning of a commitment to a total turnaround. But although communicating change to those around you may be the easiest part of your turnaround, the follow-through can be the toughest part. That's because proving the change to be true is a little more difficult. Everyone in your life will be watching and waiting to see if your behavior indeed matches your words.

When I received Christ at 16 and committed to a total turnaround, the change was recognizable. My friends quickly realized I was serious about the decisions I made for myself because my actions proved my words to be true. Not only had I made a decision in the privacy of my home but my choices were publicly seen and heard as well. People no longer heard vulgar language coming from my mouth, and they didn't see me running around with the same group of guys. They saw my choice just as clearly as they heard my choice.

In Acts 4, Peter and John are arrested and brought before the council for questioning concerning their teaching and healing in Jesus's name. Even though the religious leaders are nonbelievers, they cannot deny these men's likeness to Christ. Acts 4:13 says, "When they saw the boldness of Peter and John, and perceived that they were uneducated, common men, they were astonished. And they recognized that they had been with Jesus."

Committing to a total turnaround will require you, as a Christ follower, to become recognizable to all who witness your walk. Your friends and enemies alike will be forced to agree that change has come to your life. They will recognize you as someone who has been with Jesus. You make the choice for your life, and Jesus will make the change in your life—a change explainable only through His power.

If it's true that somewhere between 80 and 90 percent of what humans learn is visual, then your actions definitely speak louder than your words. People are watching you whether or not you realize it, and you may never know the impact you have on someone's life just by your walking closely with Jesus. Skeptics and nonbelievers often pay closest attention when a Christian is walking through a tough season. Therefore, I challenge you to live a life that will merit influencing others to follow Christ in all circumstances.

Because you are human, you won't get it right every time. Difficult circumstances will knock you clear off your feet—a shocking diagnosis, a wayward child, an unforeseen financial burden, an excruciating loss, a heartbreaking betrayal… The list goes on. But while you can't always determine what happens to you, you can decide to lead and respond with love. You can choose to lean into Jesus when everything about your situation tells you to lean into worldly comforts instead. People will be watching every step of the way. Will they recognize you as someone who has been with Jesus?

Committing to a total turnaround—whether in your life as a whole or in one particular area—will open the door for God to defy the odds against you. When you surrender every area to Him and daily choose to pursue His will above all else, God will show up in ways you never thought possible and create opportunities you would never consider. He never wastes anything given to Him. He will use every aspect of your life to further His kingdom, but that requires you to get off the fence and become recognizable. If you commit to Him, He will create a total turnaround.

4

FEAR CAN STEAL YOUR FUTURE

C hristians at a high point in their walk with the Lord are often described as being "on fire for God." That's because of the excitement they can't seem to contain. After I got saved, I was definitely on fire for God in every way. I was so excited about what He had done that I wanted to tell everyone. I couldn't talk about my salvation without having a huge smile on my face. I wanted everyone to know God could do for them what He had done for me.

We started attending church in Manchester. But it was such a long drive every Sunday, and we felt like we needed to find a church closer to home. Around this time, a relative of my mother's died, and a pastor named Ralph Shrum preached the funeral. Mama leaned over to me after the service and said, "We need to go to his church in McMinnville."

The next week we found ourselves attending McMinnville Congregational Methodist Church, a tiny cement-block building on Cadillac Lane. A highly attended Sunday service might have included 30 or so people. Pastor Ralph was a handsome young preacher who was always well dressed and never had a hair out of place, and he also really loved the Lord. The church was small and simple, but God used this little building and its pastor to put me on a path for a future I couldn't have planned for myself.

I had become so interested in reading my Bible, and I was hungry to study it and learn more about God. Pastor Ralph also told me I needed to follow the Lord in believer's baptism, so we picked the Sunday. Everyone who got baptized in our area went down to this one part of Collins River known as the Ice Hole. I remember stepping into that water on the day of my baptism thinking its name was definitely fitting; the water was as cold as ice. Yet its temperature didn't take away my joy and the excitement I felt about getting baptized. The Ice Hole didn't affect my being on fire for God.

The Makings of a Preacher

Not long after I was baptized, I turned 17. I certainly wasn't telling anyone this (no one in our family had ever been a preacher), but I felt like I was supposed to preach. The only time most of my family members showed up in a church was either to attend someone's funeral or be there for their own. Plus, I didn't want to be a preacher anyway; it couldn't have been further from any plan I had considered for my life. I watched the TV show *Perry Mason* growing up, and I had always thought being a lawyer would be a great job. I wanted to sue 'em, not save 'em!

The thought of standing in front of a crowd of people and preaching the gospel seemed like the most terrifying thing I could ever do. Speaking in front of a crowd about anything would be enough to make me nauseous. My mother told me that when I was a child, I would run and hide under the bed in my room whenever company came over, and I was so shy that, in public, I would hide behind her legs and stare straight at my shoes when anyone came up to us.

As a teenager, then, I struggled with acne and had very little confidence in myself, so I would take an *F* on any oral assignment at school. As soon as the teacher handed them out, my heart started to race, and I knew I would probably skip school that day. My self-esteem was in the negative, so the odds of my becoming a preacher seemed nonexistent.

I kept my mouth shut about preaching and just continued studying my Bible and learning all I could about God. I carried my Bible with me to school every day and read it during my lunch period. (After all, I definitely couldn't preach from a Bible I didn't know and understand.) I also attended any prayer meetings held during the week as well as Sunday services. I was committed to developing a closer relationship with God, and I worked on that daily.

But the possibility of becoming a preacher didn't go away.

Pastor Ralph became somewhat of an inspiration for me because he wasn't a very extroverted person outside of the pulpit. In the pulpit, he was definitely on fire for God, but he seemed rather laid back and reserved when he was just talking with people. I couldn't help but consider that a shy guy like me might become a preacher one day as well, and the more I tried to not think about preaching, the more I just couldn't get the idea out of my head.

Mama told me she would hear noises coming from my room late at night like I was hollering about something. She would get up to check on me, and when she opened the door and heard what I was saying, she'd realize I was preaching in my sleep. She eventually told Pastor Ralph, "I guess Benny has done got saved and thinks he's a preacher now. He's preaching in his sleep."

"Well, let's see if he's a preacher," he responded.

I told Pastor Ralph about my feeling like I was called to preach, and because he thought I needed a chance to act on that calling, he arranged a Sunday night service to give me the opportunity. I was 17 years old and scared to death, but I guess John Wayne said it best: "Courage is being scared to death but saddling up anyway." I had never been so nervous about anything in my life, but I saddled up.

Being scared doesn't mean you shouldn't go forward; it just means you need someone stronger in your life to help you keep going, and I've learned that fear and apprehension push you to lean on God. But I had only just begun learning about Him, the Bible, and what it meant to be a Christian. As a teenage boy feeling called to preach, I probably related the most to Jeremiah, who said to the Lord, "I do not know how to speak, for I am only a youth" (Jeremiah 1:6). God responded by letting Jeremiah know He equips those He calls. He gave Jeremiah words and told him to not be afraid.

I, too, was scared and needed God to give me the words and strength to step into that pulpit and preach. I had never even stood in front of my 15 or so classmates at school much less the entire congregation of a church.

I prepared a message on Nicodemus and how Jesus said we must be born again in John chapter 3, and the Sunday night I was scheduled to preach finally arrived. I must have been shaking like a leaf on a tree as I stepped into that pulpit. I preached my entire message and everything else I knew. (I often say that I preached all I knew and even some things I didn't know.) It felt like I preached for an hour straight, but in reality my message lasted seven minutes. Seven minutes! But my preaching began right there in that little cement-block building. I just couldn't get enough of sharing the gospel after that night.

Of course, it wasn't like that seven-minute message was a success and my ministry immediately took off. No, churches weren't calling me to come preach in one of their services. I just started preaching everywhere I could, like street corners, nursing homes, and rescue missions. Mac Mulligan ran the rescue mission in our area, taking people off the streets and giving them a place to stay. He would let me come preach to the homeless. And every other Saturday I went to Twin Oaks nursing home to preach to the elderly folks there. I even traveled to speak at some churches.

One old man at the nursing home was named Avery. He took my Bible and ran off with it just about every week, so I decided to get him his own Bible. I delivered it to him one afternoon, and as I was leaving, I heard a commotion coming from his room. He and his roommate had started fighting over the Bible to determine who would get to keep it.

I went back to preach two weeks later and found Avery sitting on the front porch steps with a friend and the Bible, so I guessed he had won the fight. He was holding it upside down and talking as if he was reading. As I got closer to the steps, I heard him say to his buddy, "Thou shalt not smoke."

Of course, the Bible doesn't say that. But the friend leaned over and said, "But, Avery, you smoke."

Avery responded rather quickly. "Yeah, but that's not for me; it's for you."

I think that's how a lot of people are. They think certain Scriptures are for certain people but not for them.

Preaching at the nursing home and the rescue mission was an important season in my life. God taught me that He's more interested in my availability than my ability. People often tell me they've been asking God to use them, and my response is always the same: "Just get usable, and then God will wear you out." Ephesians 2:10 says, "We are his workmanship, created in Christ Jesus for good works, which God prepared beforehand, that we should walk in them." God has created you for a purpose, and He's already given you the ability to do good works. You just have to start right where you are and make yourself available. God makes each person a unique individual and puts a unique passion in each one.

My passion was preaching, and at 17 years of age, I had found what I truly loved to do. But the odds of my becoming a successful preacher were not at all good. Earning a living as a preacher was uncommon in the mountains of Tennessee. Most of them in our area had a second or third job to supplement their ministry income, so I knew choosing that path would lead to many obstacles. But regardless of the odds, I was blown away that God would use a guy like me in the first place, and I just couldn't see myself doing anything else. I allowed God to use me right where I was, and I left it up to Him to take me elsewhere.

I hope you understand the big difference between success and significance. Success has to do with you, but significance has to do with others. The world views success by what you gain, while significance is measured by the impact your life has on other people. At a young age I knew my life was supposed to be about other people. I was so excited about the Lord, and I wanted everyone to experience salvation. I wasn't the smartest or most talented—I was best described as high energy and low IQ!—but I was eager and obedient.

I preached during my senior year of high school, and I continued taking my Bible to school. Many kids would make fun of me in class, in the hallways, and at the lunch tables. In the bathroom between classes, some boys filled a sink with water and said, "The sink is full of water, preacher boy. Why don't you come walk on it?" I didn't have many friends after I got saved because I wasn't the same person and I couldn't hang out with the same people. I wasn't willing to compromise who I was in Christ for a little fun with friends.

Once someone asked me if Christians can still sin, and I answered, "Christians can sin; they just can't sin and enjoy it." Being a Christian at school and a lot of other places wasn't easy, but I knew I was called to preach, and I didn't intend to let any obstacles get in my way.

I also got a job at a local business, Carpet Beauty. I was a janitor, and I cleaned bathrooms. I went to school for half a day, worked in the afternoon, and then preached whenever I had the opportunity. On rare free afternoons, I went to Sonic for a burger and Coke with my friend Terry, and then we rode around town eating and talking about life. He was definitely a lot different from the friends I had before getting saved, and having only one friend was fine with me. I didn't have much time for friends between school, work, and preaching.

Then one day a few people from our area who planned to start a church came to see me. They wanted me to be their pastor.

An Official Opportunity

It sounds like such a great honor to be a sought-after preacher at 17, but that wasn't exactly the case in my situation. You see, these people had a disagreement with their old church and then decided to start a new one. When it came to a pastor, they simply stated, "We'll take whatever preacher we can get," and they got me! The salary was absolutely nothing, but I was proud to pastor my very first church.

Mountain Crest Church began in the unfinished basement of Shirley Jones's house. Shirley ran a body shop out of his basement during the week, but on weekends he moved the cars out to set up chairs for Sunday service, with about 15 people in attendance. Mama always came. When I'd traveled to churches to preach, she'd always been in the audience supporting me, and she certainly wasn't going to miss me preaching at my own church.

While it may have been a tiny congregation, Mountain Crest was filled with faithful people who loved the Lord. And even though I was a basement pastor with no salary, I was right where God wanted me.

After about five months in the body shop basement, our little congregation decided to build a church on Harrison Ferry Mountain. The church was a white, cement-block building. We had to separate into the four corners of one big room for Sunday school classes, using folding chairs. Then we'd come back together to sit in the pews for worship. The only other rooms were the restrooms on either side of the entrance.

In this little church I continued preaching everything I knew and some things I didn't know. I didn't have a lot of knowledge, but I was doing my best. I laugh about it now, but I used to preach from the book of Psalms and pronounce it "Pisms." And one day a lady in the church approached me and asked, "What does epistles mean in the Bible?" I explained, "The epistles are the apostles' wives."

Remember, I was high energy and low IQ. I was just learning as I was going, but I was being obedient right where God had me.

Because of the choices I'd made in the past, people didn't believe it when they heard I was preaching. A classmate of mine reacted by saying, "And I'm a flying nun!" I wasn't surprised by her response; the life I'd lived wouldn't have led anywhere near the front doors of a church much less into a pulpit. But God had already defied so many odds in my life, and He continued to grow me as a pastor in that tiny church on Harrison Ferry Mountain for a little over a year.

God used me—a terrified kid—to preach the gospel because I simply refused to let fear steal my future. And with almost 40 years of ministry behind me as I write, not much has changed. Yet I've been fearful along the way. Numerous circumstances have caused fear to rise up and attempt to keep me from doing God's will. And for many years, fearful situations caused me to struggle with guilt.

I would read the beginning of 1 John 4:18 and feel incredibly guilty, because in that verse we're told, "There is no fear in love, but perfect love casts out fear." I thought fear in my life meant I wasn't loving God enough. I thought my love for Him wasn't perfect enough to drive out fear. But as I studied His Word and grew in my walk with Him, I began to realize I was understanding that verse all wrong.

My love for God isn't what that verse is talking about; it's talking about God's love for me. Because He loves me so much and has a perfect plan for my life, I never have to fear what lies ahead. And although fear continues to rear its ugly head from time to time, I refuse to let it steal my future. God's love is too perfect, and His plans are too great.

◆

My personal experiences have shaped my belief in the necessity of simply making ourselves usable for God, and that's why I encourage you to do what you can with what you have where you are. If you do, God won't leave you where you are, and He'll increase what you have. I encourage you to start small and think tall. The greatest journey in the world begins with one step. You can go anywhere from right where you are now. Dream big and believe that God wants to do something with your life. Don't let fear creep in and stop you from following His plan.

Your number one enemy, Satan, is no dummy when it comes to deceiving people, but he isn't too diverse in his schemes. Fear is one of his main go-to tactics when he's trying to keep lost people from experiencing salvation and keep Christians from following God. Satan knows creating fear in your heart will lead to other struggles, such as living with doubt and anxiety. Fear can breed a multitude of problems that keep you from becoming all that God created you to be.

If you find yourself battling a fearful situation or drowning from the weight of fears that have accumulated over time, I encourage you to seek the freedom and peace that comes only from closeness with God. His perfect love is strong enough to cast out every fear that seeks to control you. Inviting the Holy Spirit into your life and allowing Him to guide your words, thoughts, and actions in every moment will help you face your fears head-on and become victorious in defeating Satan's attempts to keep you from the life you were created to live.

When you begin living in the truth that God is bigger than any fear you will ever face, He can defy the odds in your life despite your fear. And to begin seeing victory over fear, I believe you must face your fears, familiarize your fears, and fight your fears.

Face Your Fears

Have you ever seen someone jump at a scary or intense moment in a movie and then quickly explain why they reacted that way? They follow up with, "I wasn't scared; I was just…" Then they give one of a variety of excuses. People have a tendency to cover their fears with excuses to legitimize how they're feeling or responding. Instead of admitting fear, they provide an excuse for the response that's actually a direct result of their fear.

Common responses to fearful situations are running, hiding, and freezing. The same three responses can occur in your walk with Christ. When faced with fearful situations, you may try to run away from God's presence, hide from God's conviction, or freeze in following God's plan. While it's human nature to avoid whatever causes you fear, letting the Holy Spirit direct your steps in fearful situations is the only way to experience peace. But you must face your fears before you can give them to God, and then you must hand them over to Him with no intention of taking them back.

You will never truly face your fears as long as you make excuses for how you respond to fear. Whether you experience common fears such as the fear of financial burden, rejection, or failure, you must not make excuses for your responses. Fearing financial burden may keep you from giving freely to the Lord, but you excuse it as financial planning. Fear of rejection may keep you from creating relationships and sharing Jesus with others, but you excuse it as an introverted personality trait. Failure is a common fear that can keep you from trying new things or stepping out of your comfort zone, but you say you have too much on your plate to start anything new.

Whatever the fearful situation may be, your excuses will probably sound legitimate to you and to others. But even though they sound good, they ignore a problem that will only deepen its roots over time.

In Acts 9, God directed Ananias toward Damascus to bring healing to a dangerous man. Everyone, including Ananias, knew Saul's reputation for killing Christians. Ananias voiced his concerns, but God reassured him of His plan. Ananias didn't run from his assignment like Jonah did, he didn't try hiding from God like Adam and Eve did, and he didn't freeze by refusing to go where directed like ten of Moses's spies did. He stated his fear to God but continued to be obedient.

Overcoming fear begins with acknowledging what frightens you. Don't continue making excuses for your responses to fear; when you do, you're giving more ground to the Enemy. Instead, face your fears and communicate them honestly to God. Only then will you experience deliverance and victory from the weight fear places on your shoulders. There is no shame in being fearful. Fear is normal. You just can't let it have control over your life.

Familiarize Your Fears

Once you face your fears and refuse to let them control your life, you must let them know who's boss. Familiarize your fears with your God. Communicate that He is greater and stronger than anything you face. Speaking God's Word and truth over what frightens you will provide you with a lasting strength and a heavenly perspective.

David's proclamation to the Philistine giant in 1 Samuel 17 is the perfect example of familiarizing your fears with your God. When he approached Goliath on the battlefield, he refused to let fear consume him as the giant laughed and mocked his youth and size. Instead, David responded by stating, "You come to me with a sword and with a spear and with a javelin, but I come to you in the name of the Lord of hosts, the God of the armies of Israel, whom you have defied. This day the Lord will deliver you into my hand, and I will strike you down and cut off your head" (1 Samuel 17:45-46). David not only faced his fear but familiarized Goliath with God's power and truth.

If you're not careful, you'll continually focus on the details of your circumstances and accept them as truth for the outcome. But in reality, your circumstances never factor in the promises of God and the power of His presence. When you are faced with difficulty, fear may begin to overwhelm you, but the truth is fear is not an indicator of failure but of a need for the Father. You can maintain a heavenly perspective by proclaiming God's Word over your life instead of accepting your circumstances as truth.

Circumstances may say funds are low and financial ruin is in your future, but Philippians 4:19 says, "God will supply every need of yours according to his riches in glory in Christ Jesus." Circumstances may say you're a failure because you didn't get the job, but Romans 8:28 says, "We know that for those who love God all things work together for good, for those who are called according to his purpose." Circumstances may say you're weak because you've given in to temptation, but 1 Corinthians 10:13 says, "No temptation has overtaken you that is not common to man. God is faithful, and he will not let you be tempted beyond your ability, but with the temptation he will also provide the way of escape, that you may be able to endure it."

Circumstances lie, and fear is simply false evidence appearing to be real. The details of your circumstances may appear true in the moment, but through the lens of Christ they hold no truth. When standing face-to-face with your fears, you must use God's Word as your weapon, because that's the only way to ensure victory. Remember that God's perfect love casts out fear, and the power of His love can overtake your strongest enemy. Tell your fears about your Father. Let them become familiar with Him, and they will begin to fade.

Fight Your Fears

David faced Goliath on the battlefield and made him familiar with God. But he didn't stop there; he acted on the truth of God's Word. If he had walked away after proclaiming God's power, the Israelites would have remained frozen in fear on that battlefield, staring across at the Philistine army.

You can know Scripture and believe it to be true, but faith requires you to walk in God's promises. James 1:22 instructs, "Be doers of the word, and not hearers only, deceiving yourselves." And in 2:17, James says, "Faith by itself, if it does not have works, is dead." Therefore, you must face your fears, proclaim God's power, but then fight your fears by pushing forward. You must walk out the promises and power of God in which you believe.

If you let fear determine your steps, you will remain still, but if you let faith determine your steps, there's no limit to where God can lead you. Yes, the first step may be terrifying, and the second step will most likely be scary, too, but obedience does not require the absence of fear. It only requires complete reliance on God. Saying yes to Him in spite of fear is faith in action.

You can believe in a chair's ability to support your weight, but you don't trust in its ability until you sit down. I often say you can believe in soap and die dirty. The same is true for your walk with Christ—the evidence of your faith will remain unseen until action is involved. God wants you to step out in faith even when circumstances are frightening, and He promises to meet your every move along the way. Satan wants you to believe there is security in remaining still. But the safest place to be is the center of God's will, and you must fight the urge to remain still by choosing to fight your fears head-on.

Following God when you're fearful will be incredibly uncomfortable because everything in your flesh will scream "No!" But if you don't push past the discomfort, you'll never progress. Stretching can be painful, but it's an indicator of growth. God will defy the odds in your life when you remain obedient to His calling no matter how fearful a situation becomes. His Word encourages and promises, "Fear not, for I am with you; be not dismayed, for I am your God; I will strengthen you, I will help you, I will uphold you with my righteous right hand" (Isaiah 41:10).

God is ready and willing to see you through, but you must first decide that you won't let fear steal your future.

A POSITIVE PERSPECTIVE

During my time as pastor of Mountain Crest Church, my mother began a relationship with a Canadian man named Don Mason. He was such a good person, the greatest man in my mother's life out of all her relationships. She ended up marrying Don, and I was privileged to officiate their wedding. He was the first man in all of our lives who provided love and encouragement. He saw the best in us and always spoke with kindness and optimism.

I finished my senior year of high school and graduated—just barely. I hadn't made good grades, and I didn't receive any honors at the graduation ceremony. I often joke how I was in the bottom half of my class that made the top half possible. Mama would get so mad about my grades. She'd shout, "Benny, these grades are terrible! Look at these pathetic grades."

One time my sister spoke up, saying, "Well, there is a good side to this, Mama."

Mama snapped back, "Good side? *D*s, *F*s… The very best he's doing is a *C*. What is the good side to this?"

Rhonda said, "At least we know he isn't cheating." I certainly hadn't been cheating, and my report cards were proof. But somehow I had done just enough to get by and graduate. I didn't know what I would do next. I had been too busy with school, work, and preaching to think about any clear steps after graduation.

Don's Confidence in Me

One day Don asked me what I was planning to do with my life. As if my current job was what I would be doing for the rest of my days, I told him I was working as a janitor, making $3.30 an hour. Not until I was older did I truly realize where you are right now doesn't determine your destiny; you don't have to stay where you are. Don knew that back then, and he saw giftedness in me. I just didn't see it in myself.

He said, "Benny, I have heard you preach many times, and you have a special gift. I believe in you."

No man had ever told me anything like that, but God used Don to speak words of encouragement to me. There is power in our believing in someone, and never underestimate the power of speaking words of encouragement into someone's life. I can't help but think about how powerful it was for Barnabas to believe in Paul in Acts 9. He stood up for Paul when others questioned his conversion. He made such an impact with his words that others changed his name to something that better reflected his character. Acts 4:36 tells us his name was Joseph, but he was given the nickname Barnabas, which means "son of encouragement." There is so much power in our words.

Don, an entrepreneur who did very well for himself by selling sheet metal and siding for homes, showed just how much he believed in me. He said if I enrolled in Bible college, he would pay my tuition for every degree I pursued. I was overwhelmed. No one had ever believed in me the way he did, and no one had ever wanted to see me succeed the way he did. I couldn't believe the opportunity he was placing before me.

But I didn't believe in myself. I tried explaining to Don that I hadn't done very well in school; I had struggled to pass every single grade level. I will never forget his response: "You just get enrolled. I'll pay for it. If you don't make it, then I'm the one losing the money. You have nothing to lose." He was willing to risk his money to invest in my future.

I enrolled at Covington Theological Seminary and was filled with so much apprehension, wondering how I would ever complete a college degree. I worked all day as a janitor at Carpet Beauty and attended Bible college at night. I worked as hard as I could, and Don encouraged me along the way. In a little over eight years, I earned an associate's degree, a bachelor's degree, a master's degree, and a doctoral degree. Don kept his word and paid for it all, even though he passed away before I was able to complete every degree. He left money specifically for Mama to continue paying for my education. I've saved several of my grade reports from my time in Bible college, and I earned four degrees while making straight As.

There was such a difference between my grade-school report cards and my college grade reports because of the difference between the man who told me I would never amount to anything and the stepfather who told me I could achieve anything. Many times I've sat in my office looking at those diplomas on the wall, thinking about how Bill, my abuser, was so wrong.

In 1 Samuel 16, we read how even David's father didn't believe in him; Jesse presented every other son to Samuel (seven total) before he ever thought to present David. When everyone else saw a little shepherd boy, God saw a king. The truth is there is a king or queen in every one of us. I'm so thankful for Don's belief in me. When everyone else saw only a poor boy from the wrong side of the tracks, he saw a preacher. Encouragement truly makes all the difference.

I'm so thankful for what God says about me, and He brought Don into my life at just the right time to speak words of encouragement and to believe in me when I didn't believe in myself. Don motivated me to take the first step, and God gave me the ability to defy every odd stacked against me in college. To this day, I attribute so much of my success to Don's believing in me. He passed away when I was 26 years old, and I now wear the stones from his Masonic ring in my wedding band as a daily reminder to encourage and invest in others as often as I can. That's exactly what Don did for me.

As I went through Bible college, I ended my time at Mountain Crest Church and began traveling to other churches, preaching wherever I was invited. My home church was still McMinnville Congregational Methodist pastored by Ralph Shrum, and he would ask me to preach there from time to time as well. Mama and I had become really good friends with Pastor Ralph and his wife, Nellie, over the years, and our families spent a lot of time together.

The Girl of My Dreams

I was 19 years old and spent all of my time working, attending Bible college, and preaching. I didn't have many friends, and I certainly didn't have a girlfriend. As a matter of fact, I'd never had a girlfriend. I was so insecure that I didn't think any girl would be interested in me. I never saw myself being able to marry a really pretty girl, either, because I didn't consider myself handsome. I had no self-esteem.

A good, godly girl, then, was all I expected and wanted. Ministry can be tough and extremely draining, and I needed a wife who would pray for me and encourage me in the Lord through every season of my ministry. But I knew my past reputation wouldn't attract Christian girls whose parents would agree to their dating me, so the chances of my finding a godly girl who would see me for what I was becoming, not only what I had been, were pretty low. But God had already defied the odds in my life in so many amazing ways, so I remained faithful in praying for that godly girl.

As I prayed daily for God to send me a wife who would make me a better person and a better preacher by always pointing me to Jesus, little did I know that a really pretty godly girl was praying, *God, send me a man who will go to church with me.*

S. Truett Cathy once said the three most important decisions you'll ever make are who your master will be, who your mate will be, and what your mission will be.[1] At 19, I had already made two of those three big decisions. I knew my master and my mission, but I hadn't yet decided on my mate. And I had to choose her carefully because I knew my wife would make or break me in ministry. Lifelong decisions can be easier to make if you've determined clear values, and I often encourage young people to establish theirs early in life so major decisions will be made with more clarity.

While sitting in a doctor's waiting room in Tracy City, Tennessee, with my mother, I laid eyes on the girl who would one day become my wife. Of course, I didn't know that in the moment. All I knew was the beautiful brunette sitting across the waiting room and flipping through a high school yearbook was someone with whom I wanted to strike up a conversation. But I was so timid and shy, and I had no clue how to get her attention.

With a deep breath and a turning stomach, I finally crossed the waiting room, planning to ask her if I could see the yearbook when she was finished with it—even though I didn't care about it one bit. I only cared about a chance to talk to her. I may have stumbled through my question because of nervousness, but she looked up at me with her dark-brown eyes and said, "Here. You can look at it right now." She handed me the yearbook, and then she got up and walked out the door of the doctor's office. I stood in that waiting room holding the yearbook thinking, *That did not go as planned.*

As I returned to my seat, I realized the girl's mother was still there. She was waiting to pick up a pair of glasses for her husband, and she had witnessed my encounter with her daughter. She introduced herself to my mother and me. Mrs. Rennice Roberts told us a little about herself and her daughter, Barbara. Much to my surprise, that beautiful dark-eyed girl who'd caught my eye was very sick. Her mother explained that she'd started having terrible seizures multiple times a day at age 18. She struggled through daily routines and took 13 pills a day just to manage her seizures as best as possible. My heart became heavy for a stranger that day.

A week or so passed, and I just couldn't get my mind off of that beautiful, sick girl. I spoke to Pastor Ralph about her, and I told him I felt the need to pray for her every day, asking God to heal her of those seizures. He was shocked when he heard me mention a girl much less show a great deal of interest in one. I had never shared my interest in any girls with anyone, not even with my mother.

Pastor Ralph and his wife, Nellie, began playing matchmaker behind my back. They knew Barbara through the pastor of her church and began mentioning my name to her whenever they saw her. We laugh about it now, but Barbara couldn't even remember anything specific about what I looked like when Nellie mentioned our encounter at the doctor's office. I didn't make much of a first impression, and she wasn't all that interested in meeting me, but Nellie was adamant that I was a good, godly boy Barbara just had to meet.

After their several failed attempts at trying to get us together in the same place, I finally called Barbara myself and asked her on a date. She may have remembered me only as a skinny boy from the doctor's office, but she said yes to dinner. She was the prettiest girl I had ever laid eyes on, and I couldn't believe someone like her would say yes to a guy like me. Regardless, I was taking Barbara Roberts to Captain D's that Friday night.

We went on two or three dates, and I was head over heels in love. Some people say that's puppy love, but it's real to the dogs! After only three short months, I felt like I had known Barbara my entire life, and I knew for certain that I wanted to marry her. She was the answer to my prayers for a mate, and I guess I was the answer to her prayers too. She'd been praying for God to send her a husband who would go to church with her; she just had no idea He would send her a pastor.

I often tell people I out-punted my coverage when I married Barbara. God sent me not only a godly girl but an extremely pretty girl. He really was defying the odds in every area of my life.

Barbara and I had talked about marriage many times, and she believed we were meant to be together. The only thing standing in the way of our engagement was her father's blessing, and I had to ask Mr. Roberts for her hand in marriage. Would he say yes because he knew how much we loved each other? Or would he say no because of my checkered past? I wasn't at all sure of his answer.

Talking to Mr. Roberts was more stressful than proposing to Barbara. I was so nervous, and I'm sure I stumbled all over the question. But his response stunned me: "I don't recommend it. You're young and healthy, and she has as many as ten seizures a day. You don't know what you're getting into medically or financially, son. You won't be able to live a normal life. I suggest you get into your car, get off this mountain, and don't come back."

My jaw immediately dropped. Leave and never come back… Really? I couldn't even gather my thoughts before responding, "But I love your daughter. I understand that she has seizures, but that doesn't change how I feel about her. I want to spend the rest of my life with her." I was prepared to drop to my knees and beg him for approval if that's what it took. I could feel tears making their way to my eyes ready to fall at his definite no.

Her daddy finally agreed to give me her hand in marriage, and Barbara said yes to my proposal. It seemed that everything was falling perfectly in place. We were two young kids so in love and not at all worried about the obstacles in our future. Our excitement for marriage was high, but the odds for success were low. Mr. Roberts was right about one thing: I was young and naive about what the future held for us as a married couple. But we set the date for our wedding—July 3, 1984.

It was a roller-coaster ride leading up to the big day. Her family was concerned about my past, Barbara called off the wedding the night before, her father refused to attend and walk her down the aisle, and there was very little money for the ceremony. It was a rough start to say the least, but our wedding day turned out better than we ever hoped.

Barbara walked down the aisle in the prettiest $35 wedding dress I had ever seen. I stood by Pastor Ralph in my new gray suit paired with the biggest smile possible, and I was the happiest man on the planet. Looking back at our wedding photos, we look like two kids playing dress-up. I often say we were so young that we didn't know whether to go on a honeymoon or to summer camp. But at 19, I was a married man with a beautiful bride and all the optimism in the world.

Encouragers

Married life was certainly an adjustment for us both, but we were so excited to begin our life together. Barbara was a constant encourager to me, and her faith challenged me to trust God more in every area of life. She spoke words of encouragement to me daily and prayed over my ministry, our family, and our future. God had given me exactly what I needed—a godly wife with a positive perspective.

Mark Twain once said, "I can live on a good compliment two weeks with nothing else to eat."[2] I believe the same is true for most people—everyone responds to praises and raises. I often say that everyone is walking around with an invisible sign hanging around their neck that says "Make me feel good about myself." Between the world's negativity and personal insecurities tearing people down, kind words of encouragement can mean eternity for someone's life. God uses people to communicate hope and love in times of weakness.

I am so grateful for the people God placed in my life over the years who spoke words of encouragement to me—great or small. Many times the compliments and encouragement were all that got me through tough times before I came to know Christ. As a young boy growing up in a dysfunctional home, I really could live for weeks off of a person's kind words. Praise received from a teacher or coach meant more to me than anything else, because no one at home was pouring into me with positive words of affirmation.

As a kid, I played Little League baseball for many years, but one year in particular had an enormous impact on my life. Ronnie Watson was somewhat famous in our league because he recruited the best players and had the best team. While I was never one of his recruits, he made a difference in my life more than any other coach. I was playing third base one season when our team played against Coach Watson's. One of his players hit a ground ball to me at third base, and I fielded the ball and threw his runner out at first. Coach Watson couldn't holler or clap for me, but he softly said where only I could hear, "Good play, little man." That one whispered compliment from the best coach in the league impacted me for life.

A framed collage of meaningful words, phrases, and names that have impacted me over the years hangs in my office. One of the phrases printed in bold reads "Good play, little man." It serves as a reminder that encouragement of the smallest kind can mean so much. Ronnie Watson had no idea the amount of life he was speaking into a little third baseman who craved recognition and affirmation.

The same is true for Don Mason, who believed in my ability to succeed in Bible college. And the same is true for Barbara, who has supported and encouraged me throughout the highs and lows of life. The words of encouragement and positive perspectives shared by many others over the years have gotten me through some of the most difficult times. Sharing positivity is worth so much to the recipient while costing nothing to the giver.

God can defy the odds in your life when you maintain a positive perspective and commit to encouragement. I understand that a variety of issues create negativity and division in society today, making it difficult to maintain a positive perspective. And when your focus is on the things of this world, little positivity and encouragement will be found. Yet you can maintain a positive perspective, be a constant encourager, and share hope when you keep your eyes on Jesus and on others.

Eyes on Jesus

In Matthew 22:37-38, Jesus said, "You shall love the Lord your God with all your heart and with all your soul and with all your mind. This is the great and first commandment." Positivity, encouragement, and hope will be impossible unless Jesus is your number one focus. All good things flow from God alone. If your eyes are fixed on something or someone else, situations and relationships will always remain out of order. To keep your eyes firmly fixed on the Lord, you must know Him and praise Him.

Know Him

God has always been your Father because He created you. Jesus becomes your Savior with a decision, but He becomes your Lord through a process. I often say some of us want just enough of Jesus to get out of hell, but we need enough of Jesus to get the hell out of us. Knowing God intimately is an ongoing process. Only then can you maintain a positive perspective in a world filled with darkness.

Having a deep understanding of who God is and knowing His character allows you to endure whatever life throws at you with unwavering faith. God is too good to be unkind and too wise to be mistaken.

When you can't trace His hand, you can trust His heart. That is definitely easier said than done when you find yourself facing life's darkest moments, but you must pursue God and study His Word daily in order to form a strong foundation before the hardships come. Knowing God's character and trusting His heart will allow you to maintain a positive perspective as well as give encouragement and share hope in the most violent storms of this life.

Praise Him

God deserves every bit of your praise even when circumstances seem terrible. Praising Him through your darkest moments will allow you to see beyond your immediate situation and recognize His goodness in all things. Acts 16 is a wonderful example of praising God in the midst of trouble.

Paul and Silas were wrongly accused, beaten, and thrown into prison, yet they chose to praise God in the middle of their storm. Acts 16:25 says, "About midnight Paul and Silas were praying and singing hymns to God, and the prisoners were listening to them." The prison walls shook and their chains broke because of their praises to God. They chose to hold tightly to what they knew to be true—God always makes a way.

The fall of Jericho in Joshua 6 is another example of the power of praise. Joshua's men and seven priests walked around the walls of Jericho for six days, but on the seventh day, they lifted their voices in praise and saw the walls come down around the city. Joshua 6:20 says, "The people shouted, and the trumpets were blown. As soon as the people heard the sound of the trumpet, the people shouted a great shout, and the wall fell down flat, so that the people went up into the city, every man straight before him, and they captured the city." God's power came down from heaven as His people lifted their voices in praise to Him. And here's the thing: The same power that brought down walls in the Bible will come down in your life as well. Praise is a magnet for God's presence.

God's power will fall in a mighty way when you begin praising Him in all circumstances. He can defy the odds in your life when you continually praise all He has done. Don't reserve your praise for times of victory; praise Him even in the battle, expecting victory.

Eyes on Others

In Matthew 22:39, Jesus gives us His second greatest command: "You shall love your neighbor as yourself." Jesus taught that our primary focus should be God but that our next priority should be loving others.

Nowhere in Scripture did Christ instruct us to focus primarily on ourselves. You are guaranteed disappointment if your eyes remain on your own circumstances. In order to maintain a positive perspective and be a person who shares hope, you must love others the way Jesus commanded. When you love people unconditionally, offer forgiveness, and show them mercy, it becomes hard to stay negative toward them. Your perspective will remain positive when your attention is directed toward bragging on others and building them up.

Brag on Them

Most people don't have a problem thinking of compliments. They may walk through a crowded space and think several positive things about those around them. But many people do struggle with verbalizing those compliments. Regardless of discomfort, never be stingy with showing appreciation and sharing accolades.

I certainly did not grow up in a culture of sharing appreciation. I rarely heard the words *Good job*. In the hills of Tennessee, a boss showed appreciation by giving you a paycheck instead of firing you. But when I became a full-time pastor and began leading a staff, I realized I needed to push beyond what was comfortable and familiar in order to brag on my team, show them appreciation, and build them up.

When you purpose in your heart to brag on others daily, you'll also find it difficult to have a negative perspective about your own circumstances. Giving flowers to others always leaves a fragrance in your own hand. By complimenting and encouraging others, you teach your brain a healthy habit. Bragging on others regularly and expressing appreciation to those with whom you come in contact will not only impact them but help you maintain a positive perspective regardless of your circumstances.

Build Them Up

The average person's life is filled to the brim with activities and appointments. We run here and there until we're completely out of breath. So our time is precious, and we find ways to expedite certain things to make room for others. The thing we often expedite most is intentional, quality time with people. We shoot a text message to make quick contact without having to engage in a full conversation. We scroll through social media accounts to see the highlight reel of peoples' lives instead of scheduling time to sit down and share with them. Many of our relationships have become hurried and distant.

While our fast-paced society may leave little room for being intentional and investing in others, the Bible says we are one body working together for the Lord. Colossians 3:16 states, "Let the word of Christ dwell in you richly, teaching and admonishing one another in all wisdom, singing psalms and hymns and spiritual songs, with thankfulness in your hearts to God." We must have a personal relationship with God's Word in order to grow spiritually as well as to minister to others. Intentionally using your time to invest in others is a priceless act of generosity. Money and objects can be regained, but time cannot. It can be spent only once.

The commonly used idiom "Actions speak louder than words" is vitally important to caring for and about people. Saying "I support you" is encouraging, but showing up to support someone means you're invested in their life. Make time in your busy schedule to invest in the lives of others. Choose to show up to the main event instead of merely commenting on the photos posted on social media later.

I am so thankful that Don Mason never stopped encouraging me in my calling to preach but was willing to put his money where his mouth was. He supported my education so I could become the best pastor I could be. He bragged on my ability to preach while also building me up through investing in my future. Don's support influenced me to always be someone who shows up. Every morning I ask myself,

Who can I help today? I want to speak words of encouragement to those around me and build up others in any way I can.

When you purpose in your heart to keep your eyes fixed on Jesus and others, God will do a transforming work without your even realizing it. When you continually praise Him and love others, He will defy the odds in your life in the most unexpected places. You'll find yourself effortlessly maintaining a positive perspective because of His good work in you.

PRAY MIRACLE PRAYERS

Barbara and I had not been married long when we realized that happily ever after looked a lot different than we'd expected. Although we were head over heels in love and so excited about our life together, very few details about our circumstances allowed us to rejoice. We were so young and so poor; we had nothing. Our home sweet home was a tiny trailer we rented fully furnished because we didn't have any furniture of our own. My uncle Sonny had secured a job for me at Tennsmith machine shop, where I made $158 a week running a milling machine, but much of the time we had very little money for groceries much less anything else.

I had contacted the hospitals about setting up payment options since there was no way I could pay the medical bills in full, and I used whatever was left of my paycheck, which wasn't much at all, to make those payments at the end of the month. At the end of the week, I also had to pay Barbara's caregivers. Because her seizures were so severe, someone had to be with her at all times. If she had a seizure in the bathtub, she could drown. If she had a seizure while cooking, the house could catch fire or she could be badly burned. She needed 24-hour care. Her seizures weren't getting any better either.

I was starting to understand what Mr. Roberts meant when he said I wasn't financially prepared for marriage to his daughter.

Before we were married, Barbara's parents had taken her to Mayo Clinic in Rochester, Minnesota, and the best doctors in the country had run every test and completed every evaluation possible to determine the cause of her seizures. Their diagnosis was that Barbara had a scar on her brain that caused the seizures, a result of either her mother falling during pregnancy or her receiving a hard hit to the head at some point.

Receiving a diagnosis was the good news. The bad news? There was no cure. The doctors informed Barbara and her parents that she would always have seizures, and they recommended she continue taking the 13 different medications daily. According to the best medical professionals in the country, she would never live a better quality of life, and severe seizures would always be a daily battle.

While I had accepted that diagnosis as truth, Barbara had not. Many nights I would wake up to the sound of her praying as she knelt beside our bed. She believed God for a miracle and faithfully prayed, "God, touch me. Heal me of these seizures." I wanted God to heal her, and I wanted to believe He would, but Barbara *knew* He would. She claimed it daily and thanked Him in advance for what He was going to do.

Romans 4:18 says, "Even when there was no reason for hope, Abraham kept hoping—believing that he would become the father of many nations. For God had said to him, 'That's how many descendants you will have!'" (NLT). Just as Abraham believed God's promises, Barbara believed God for healing. Mayo Clinic said there was no reason for hope, but Barbara kept hoping in the One who could bring healing no matter what the doctors said. She believed God to be Jehovah Rapha— the Lord who heals. Psalm 103:3 promises, "He forgives all my sins and heals all my diseases," and Barbara knew God always keeps His promises. Regardless of any medical diagnosis, she knew He could defy the odds that were stacked against her physically.

If the odds stacked against us had been only physical, I might have been more optimistic. But the odds were stacked against us emotionally and financially too. Physically, Barbara was very sick. Emotionally,

I was drained from worry. Financially, my income just wasn't enough to keep us afloat. Many weeks we couldn't afford to buy any groceries. Money was so tight that when Barbara had a seizure in public, I begged the people around us to not call an ambulance; it would be yet another bill we couldn't pay. We felt like we were drowning and could never reach a point where we would be able to keep our heads above water.

During this time God gave us a gift in the form of Delores Glenn, a precious lady who owned a little market down the street from where we lived. Many Fridays I would go into Delores's Market and explain to her that we didn't have any money but we also didn't have anything to eat. Mrs. Delores always said, "Get what you need. It will all work out." She let me get groceries on credit for the week ahead.

Years later, after I had pastored Rock Springs Church for several years, I went back to McMinnville and found Delores. I took her flowers and a gift as a small token of my appreciation, explaining just how much I valued her helping us when we were in a difficult time and that I had no idea where we would be if she had not been so generous. I know it was the providential hand of God that brought Delores into our lives to help us survive such a difficult time. She was yet another person He used to defy the odds in our life.

Never fail to show appreciation to those who help you along the way. God blesses us with situations and relationships throughout our lives to grow us and encourage us to later do the same for others. Be sure to tell those who have been instrumental in your growth and success how much you appreciate them. Then allow God to use you as instrumental in someone else's life as well.

During this scary and difficult time, I remained determined to work hard to provide for our family and pay what I could toward the bills. Barbara was faithful in praying for God to move in a mighty way. And that's just what He did.

A Miraculous Healing

Barbara came to me one day and said, "Benny, I don't have to take my medication anymore. God has healed me of my seizures." But I guess I was like the father in Mark 9:24 who said, "I believe; help my unbelief!" I was so afraid of what might happen if Barbara quit taking her medication. What if she was mistaken? What if she got worse? What if no one was with her if she had a seizure and was hurt? I couldn't agree to such a drastic change when I thought so much could go wrong. We came to the agreement that she would take her medication during the week but not on the weekends when I could be home to take care of her. While the caregivers were able to keep her from harm during the day, they weren't able to bring her out of a seizure the way I could. And without the medication, the seizures would have been worse than anything the caregivers had ever experienced.

Just a few days after our conversation, I was working at Tennsmith and talking with God as I normally did. I talked about Barbara and all that had gone on with her health issues. I said Barbara didn't have to take those pills on the weekends because I'd be home, but she needed to take them during the week while I was at work. This is one of those times I know, beyond a shadow of a doubt, that God spoke to me. His voice was so loud and clear over all the noise in that machine shop as He said, *Son, what can you do for her that I can't do?*

I immediately ran to my boss and let him know I had to go home, then I hopped into my green '79 Ford Fairmont and drove as quickly as I dared. Running up the front steps into our little house, I found Barbara standing in the kitchen, looking surprised at my being home so early. Explaining what happened at work and how I believed God had healed her, I told her she didn't have to take that medicine anymore.

Barbara quit taking all of her pills that day. In fact, she never took another one of those medications again. More than three decades have passed, and she hasn't had a single seizure!

James 5:15 says, "A prayer offered in faith will heal the sick, and the Lord will make you well" (NLT). The Lord had answered Barbara's prayers and healed her. She was made well. Mayo Clinic couldn't explain it; no one could explain it. It was a God thing, the kind of outcome where only He can receive the glory. God doesn't always heal this side of heaven, but sometimes He does. He defied the odds in Barbara's life when even the medical professionals saw no way. I'm so glad we serve a Lord and Savior who is *the Way.*

I know God's healing was for Barbara; He certainly answered her faithful prayers. But He did something in my heart through her healing as well. He knew I was going to be a pastor and that I needed faith to lift in my heart. In Matthew 9:29, Jesus said this to two blind men who believed He could make them see: "Because of your faith, it will happen" (NLT). Healing won't happen because of your family or your finances. It has nothing to do with fate but everything to do with faith. God was showing me, a young minister, that if I would trust Him for big things, He would do big things in my life.

Barbara's commitment to prayer and God's miracle healing of her also led me to realize the importance of daily prayer time. As I began dedicating more and more time to prayer, my faith was lifted. The size and depth of my prayers changed over time as I developed a strong expectation for God to do the impossible. I didn't realize it then, but God's plan for my life was leading me toward situations that would require fervent prayer and unshakeable faith.

The Unlikely Choice

During the first three years of marriage, I had traveled to preach at many different churches while also working at Tennsmith. I visited Sweeton Hill Congregational Methodist Church in Coalmont, Tennessee, several times, and I really began to feel a burden for its people. The Lord was doing great things at that little church of only 13 members, and I could sense His presence every time I was there. After Barbara's healing, I learned that Sweeton Hill's pastor had resigned and they needed someone to fill the position. I really felt that I was supposed to be their pastor, but I was a 21-year-old kid still enrolled in school, and other candidates were much more qualified.

The church invited several pastors to preach and interview for the part-time position. I expressed my interest, but I wasn't confident about being chosen. The church members finally narrowed the options to me and one other pastor—a great man and a far superior preacher with many more years of experience. Twelve members and one church leader met to cast their votes to name their next pastor.

The church leader, a man named Mandel Nunley, called to inform me I had been voted the new pastor of Sweeton Hill Congregational Methodist Church. I remember asking him about the count. His response? Simply, "You've been elected the pastor." I persistently asked a few more times before finally dragging the information out of him. "The vote was six to six," he said, "and I voted to break the tie. I sure hope you do well." As if pastoring a church at 21 wasn't stressful enough, I felt the pressure to prove that his vote had been the right one.

I was very disappointed after learning the results of the vote. I was Sweeton Hill's fourth choice, and half of the board didn't even vote in my favor. As I shared my disappointment with God, He reminded me that I may have been their fourth choice, but I was always His first choice. I want to remind you of the very same thing—whether others choose you first, last, or not at all, you are always God's first choice.

While I pastored Sweeton Hill, it grew from 13 to 300 members. Leaders of our denomination came to do a story on our church because it was one of the fastest growing churches in our denomination. The local paper even took photos and wrote articles about our unbelievable growth. God was doing an amazing work in the life of our church, but He was also doing a mighty work in my heart to develop a passion in me for reaching souls.

When I'd been at Sweeton Hill for about a year, the church had already grown so much that they decided to hire me as their first full-time pastor. Once I quit my job at Tennsmith, knocking on doors and visiting people in our community became an everyday activity for me. I wanted to take every opportunity I could to reach people for Jesus.

A drunk in our town named Frank lived a rough life. He was a lot like the people who frequented our nightclub back in the day. Frank had earned so many DUIs that he lost his driver's license and started riding a horse around town. I stopped by his house many times to invite him to church, and as we sat in his living room one day, he said, "Preacher, are you sure you want my kind in your church?" I assured him he was dearly loved and always welcome at Sweeton Hill. Before I left, Frank stopped me on the front porch and said, "Now, I'm not telling you I'm ever gonna come to your church, but I've lived in the shadow of its steeple all these years, and you're the first one to come down and invite me."

Frank had godly parents who were worried about him and continually prayed for his salvation. Many days I fasted and prayed for Frank during my lunch break. Then one night around midnight, Frank's dad called to say Frank wanted us to talk to him about God. I rushed over to Frank's house to find him quite emotional; he knew his life was in a bad place. Just as I had knelt by the couch in my living room to receive Jesus, Frank knelt by his couch and accepted the Lord that night. His transformation was a lot like my own—he immediately became a different person. Frank started attending church regularly and even got baptized.

It wasn't long until Frank became my visitation partner. We would ride around town together several days a week, knocking on doors and inviting people to church. Many of those we visited lived a rough life and knew Frank from having hung out in the same crowds. I invited them to church, and Frank would say, "If God can change me, He can change you!" People couldn't believe Frank's transformation; they never would've thought he would end up in church much less riding around with the pastor inviting others. But Frank probably led a hundred people to Christ, and he was instrumental in the tremendous growth of Sweeton Hill Church.

God used the early years of my marriage and my ministry to teach me that no situation is too dark for Him to restore. No diagnosis is too terrible or person too troubled. No obstacles are too high or burdens too heavy. Our job is to keep praying and believing while God does the rest. Barbara prayed for and believed in a miracle even though all of her doctors said healing wouldn't come. Frank's parents continued praying and believing for his salvation even though he was living deep in sin.

◆

Missionary William Carey once said, "Expect great things from God; attempt great things for God."[1] God gave me confidence through Barbara's healing. He showed me that He could do big things so I would begin to expect big things from Him. David faced Goliath after two victories over a lion and a bear, and God wanted me to expect great victories in the future because of the victories in my past. He was preparing to work miracles through my ministry, and He used Barbara's healing and Frank's salvation to build a firm foundation of faith. I could believe Him for even greater physical healings and salvation for those in the darkest valley of sin because I had already witnessed His working great miracles in those around me.

God still performs biblical-sized miracles today, but many times Christians don't see them because they either don't believe such things can happen or they simply don't ask for them.

Many years ago I heard a story about a guy who got to heaven and saw thousands of beautifully wrapped boxes stacked high in all directions. He asked Saint Peter, "What are all these beautifully wrapped boxes?" Peter explained, "These are all of the things God wanted to give people but they never asked for them."

With that story in mind, I strive to always ask God for big things. I don't want to get to heaven and see any beautifully wrapped boxes addressed to Benny Tate.

James 4:2 says, "You do not have, because you do not ask." While most Christians would say they believe that verse to be true, their thought life and personal experiences keep them from asking big. If you're going to see God do miraculous things in your life, your vision must be accurate. Your propensity to ask God for biblical-sized miracles is directly related to how you see God and how you see yourself.

How You See God

The expectations you have of God and the way you perceive His role in your life are often based on worldly standards that involve checklists and conditions commonly found in a performance-driven society. The world has a way of teaching everyone at a very early age that nothing is free and performance determines success. It can be incredibly challenging to disconnect those worldly principles from your spiritual walk. But to see miracles take place in your life, you must first consider how you see God: as a correcting God or a giving God?

A.W. Tozer boldly claimed, "What comes into our minds when we think about God is the most important thing about us."[2] While you may truly believe God to be all-powerful, it is important to identify whether you see Him as an all-powerful God who wants to correct you or an all-powerful God who wants to comfort you. Do you see Him as directing His power toward you in discipline" Or do you see Him as directing His power in delight? You won't expect God to perform biblical-sized miracles in your life if you see Him only as a disciplinarian who eagerly waits to punish your every mistake.

Seeing God as a correcting God can be a direct result of the lifelong relationship examples you've witnessed. The parental, professional, and social relationship experiences you've had throughout your life have shaped your view of Him. There are consequences for mistakes and checklists for performance in all types of relationships. Whether interacting with a parent, boss, or friend, unmet expectations result in some form of punishment. So while all other relationships in life operate this way, it can be hard to see God differently.

If you believe God's dominant traits are those of correction and discipline instead of compassion and forgiveness, you will see Him as a father who is constantly disappointed in you. You will find yourself growing distant because you feel shame for never measuring up or meeting specific standards. You may even wonder how God could love someone who messes up so much and even doubt whether He loves you at all.

Friend, I am so glad to report that God is not disappointed in you and that His focus is not one of correction and discipline. Micah 7:18-19 provides a wonderful description of God's character: "Who is a God like you, pardoning iniquity and passing over transgression for the remnant of his inheritance? He does not retain his anger forever, because he delights in steadfast love. He will again have compassion on us; he will tread our iniquities underfoot. You will cast all our sins into the depths of the sea."

God looks on you with steadfast love and compassion. He wants to give to you freely and bless you greatly. He wants to work miracles in your life for your good and His glory. You serve a God who longs to do indescribably big things in and through you. You must see Him for who He truly is and believe that He loves you unconditionally.

I understand that changing the way you view God is easier said than done. In fact, it will take time and dedication to create lasting change in seeing Him correctly. But I hope the following three practical steps will help you draw closer to the Lord and know Him better.

1. *Ask for God's wisdom:* The Bible promises that if you ask God for His wisdom, He will give it generously. Wisdom is needed for correctly interpreting and understanding God's Word. Always ask God for wisdom before reading the Bible so you don't just apply your own understanding to what you read. God's ways are higher than your ways (Isaiah 55:9); therefore, you cannot comprehend His Word without His wisdom.

2. *Look for God's character:* As you read the Bible, look for God's character in every passage you read. For example, the miracle of manna falling from heaven as described in Numbers 11 allows you to clearly see God as a provider, but you may easily overlook His precious care. God not only provided nourishment to the ungrateful Israelites but cared enough for them to provide food that was pleasing to eat. Manna was used to make delicious cakes described as tasting "like pastries baked with olive oil" (verse 8). And when the Israelites complained of having only manna, He provided them with meat. God delights in giving good things to His children; that's just one of His many characteristics seen throughout Scripture.

3. *Reflect on God's record:* The blessings of God can be seen all throughout your life, and you will see His goodness when you truly look for it. When you choose to focus on how good God has always been, your view of Him becomes clearer and more accurate. Hebrews 13:8 says, "Jesus Christ is the same yesterday and today and forever." If God has done it before, He will do it again. Let the history of God's good hand on your life lift your faith and reassure you of His promises.

How you view God will directly affect all that He does in your life. He will not force you to believe Him for big things. But when you see God accurately, you can believe Him for all He is capable of and accept all that He has in store. You will be amazed at how often God works miracles all around you when you see Him as a miracle-working God and begin praying miracle prayers.

How You See Yourself

The wrong view of God will certainly keep you from asking big and praying for miracles. Seeing yourself incorrectly, however, can also be a major obstacle in your personal prayer life. Seeing God as compassionate and forgiving will not help your prayer life if you don't view yourself as a recipient of His compassion and forgiveness.

It can be easy to fall into a pattern of thinking that God's blessings and miracles are for other people but not for you. Your view of God may be accurate, but if you don't see yourself as someone He would use or bless in certain ways, you disqualify yourself. In order to see God's miraculous work in your own life, you must determine how you see yourself: as a problem child or a prized child?

It seems as though some Christians assume Romans 3:23—"All have sinned and fall short of the glory of God"—determines their identity without continuing to read in verse 24, "and are justified by his grace as a gift, through the redemption that is in Christ Jesus." Verse 23 serves to support what society tells people daily: *You don't measure up*. People tend to be selective in what they hear and believe the worst about themselves. It's easy to begin believing there's truth in a label. Whether you've been labeled by others or have labeled yourself, your identity never comes from a label.

Trying to define yourself through your job, your appearance, your success, your financial status, or your popularity will leave you with a frail foundation, because changing circumstances will result in a continually wavering identity. You will also attach every issue to your identity and have a negative view of yourself if you don't like what you see. When you make mistakes or fail, you'll see yourself as a problem—God's problem child.

The consequences of believing that you're God's problem or burden are distance and bitterness, and then you'll grow distant from God because you feel as though you always have something bad to report or you haven't done enough to make Him proud. You begin to think you've messed up too many times or have strayed too far away for Him to love you. Then once distance has been created, bitterness toward others can grow because you think God loves them more than He loves you. Even one lying label can shift the direction of your life when you believe it to be true.

I'm so thankful that we don't have to rely on the world to determine our identity. The Bible clearly details how God sees His children. Our identity is found in Christ alone, and according to James 1:18, God "chose to give birth to us by giving us his true word. And we, out of all creation, became his prized possession" (NLT). If God sees us as His prized possession, who are we to say otherwise? We must take inventory of our thoughts and shift our negative thinking in order to clearly see ourselves the way God sees us.

You are a child of the Most High, the King of Kings. You are His prized possession, and He wants to give you the desires of your heart. He wants to bless you greatly. If you believe anything else to be true, then you're believing a lie.

In Matthew 7:11, Jesus explained, "If you then, who are evil, know how to give good gifts to your children, how much more will your Father who is in heaven give good things to those who ask him!" I understood this verse on a deeper level when I became a father, because there isn't anything in the world I wouldn't do to ensure that my daughter has everything she wants in life. I want to give her good gifts as often as possible to the best of my ability. Knowing the depth of love I have for my own child only makes me all the more grateful for the love God so freely gives to me. And He loves you just the same.

Seeing yourself correctly will always be a difficult task that must be maintained daily, because the world is quick to tell you something different. You must refresh your mind and redirect your thoughts on a regular basis to keep yourself from accepting labels as truth. These three habits can help you maintain proper vision:

1. *Claim your identity:* Frequently tell yourself whose you are—God's prized possession. Remove any other label that has remained on your life for too long and replace it with truth—you are a child of God, a joint heir with Christ.

2. *Know what God says about you:* Study the Bible to better know exactly what God thinks about you and what He has promised you. Get in His Word daily. Don't go into battle with a broken sword. Seek to know the entire Word of God that you may never fall victim to the lies of the Enemy. And memorize whole passages of Scripture—not just select verses.

3. *Change the dialogue:* Pay close attention to how you talk about yourself to others and how you talk to yourself when no one is around. Stop criticizing yourself. Don't let your struggles or shortcomings be the topic of the conversation. Instead, remind yourself and others what God is doing in your life and speak truth over your circumstances.

An incorrect view of yourself will limit what God can do in your life. Don't refuse to ask for miracles and blessings because you see yourself as unworthy of God's affection. Choose to accept all that He says about you, and claim your identity in Christ. See yourself as God's prized possession whom He longs to bless greatly.

God will defy all odds in your life when you see Him and yourself correctly. He will work miracles and pour out unimaginable blessings when you begin believing Him for big things and praying miracle prayers.

PERSISTENCE GOT THE SNAIL ON THE ARK

After 40 years of serving the Lord, I have grown to believe with certainty that God loves to use the most unlikely people to accomplish His kingdom plans. When He uses unlikely people in the most amazing ways, He alone receives all the glory. Many times people discount their ability to do great things for God because they see themselves as ordinary at best. Yet when you experience salvation and the hand of God is on your life, absolutely nothing about you is ordinary. History proves time and time again how God can use one seemingly average individual to greatly impact His kingdom for eternity.

The same is true concerning unlikely places. God loves to use them as well. After all, the Savior of the world was born in a dirty stable, welcomed and celebrated by lowly shepherds in the dark of night. While today's society often relates success to location, God relates success to expectation. You must begin expecting Him to move in a mighty way right where you are. You don't have to be in a church service to hear from God, and you don't have to be in a highly populated area to reach people for Jesus. God receives all the glory when He works in the most unlikely places. And in 1990, God called me to a seemingly unlikely place.

A Georgia Calling

One day I was told a missionary from Rock Springs Church in Milner, Georgia, was coming to visit us at Sweeton Hill. It seemed like the biggest coincidence that I was already scheduled to preach a three-night revival there. By that point, though, I should have known nothing is ever a coincidence with God. Here's what happened:

Barbara's brother had been looking for a church to pastor, and being single, he could travel anywhere for a position. Rock Springs Church had posted an advertisement in our monthly denominational magazine about seeking a pastor to preach an upcoming revival but also about being in the process of finding a new full-time pastor. When he called about the opportunity to preach the revival, the church leader asked if he had any formal Bible education. He didn't, so they didn't offer him the opportunity.

As I thought about the opportunity to preach a revival in Georgia, however, I decided to call and see if they would have me, someone who did have formal Bible education. I had never preached in Georgia, but I thought it would be a neat experience to visit there. I just had no intentions of leaving Tennessee. We loved our community and our church, we were close to both of our families, and my ministry at Sweeton Hill was successful. There was no reason for me to even consider going anywhere else much less move to Georgia.

In March of 1990, I preached the revival at Rock Springs Church. When we arrived at the church Thursday evening, I walked into the little sanctuary filled with wooden pews and green shag carpet, and I told Barbara how happy I was to see altars down front. I preached that night and thought the service went really well. I preached again on Friday night, and after the service concluded, Barbara said she felt like we were supposed to be at Rock Springs Church. My immediate response was no because I didn't feel that way. But I often say husbands miss 50 percent of what the Lord is trying to tell them if they don't listen to their wives.

Focusing on preaching and not on what Barbara said, I preached the Saturday night revival service and then again on Sunday morning. Everything had gone extremely well considering there were only around 25 to 30 people in attendance. But then we pulled out of the church parking lot in my little Dodge truck, and when we got to the end of Rock Springs Road, I stopped, laid my head on the steering wheel, and began crying. I said, "Barbara, I'm willing to come here. I don't want to, but I believe it's the Lord's will."

Once we returned home to Coalmont, I couldn't stop thinking about the Lord calling me to Rock Springs Church. I called the church and asked them to take a vote to see if the people wanted me as their pastor. When they called me back just a few days later, it was pretty clear what the people wanted. The vote was 19 to zero in my favor. It was the best vote I had ever received, but I just couldn't see how I could leave a church of 300 to pastor a church of 30—and that was on a good Sunday.

Leaving a successful church where I was comfortable made no sense in my mind, but many years in ministry have taught me that God doesn't call us to comfort; He calls us to a cross. I've heard it said that the life pleasing to God is often painful and difficult. Leaving our church family and our own families was not at all an easy task, but we knew God had called us, and I had learned the lesson of obeying God's call.

My three years spent pastoring Sweeton Hill Congregational Methodist Church were such a special time in my life. God allowed me to develop precious relationships with many people, learn valuable leadership lessons, and grow my faith in Him. Little did I know that He would orchestrate events in my future that would lead to unimaginable relationships, prestigious leadership opportunities, and gigantic faith.

Time and again in my 25 years of lifetime God had already defied the odds through unlikely salvations, miracle healings, and providential blessings. He had defied so many odds in those hills of Tennessee, but now He'd called me to Georgia, where the odds against me would be stacked higher. Yet His works would be even greater.

At the time, Milner was a tiny, rural town about an hour south of Atlanta with a population of 321. I left a church in the hills of Tennessee with a congregation that same size to pastor in a town I often describe as having the zip code E-I-E-I-O. It was definitely an unlikely place, all 2.2 square miles of it.

The incredibly small population seemed to be the greatest odd stacked against us in terms of reaching people for Jesus. And I didn't know we would become aware of even greater odds within a short time after our arrival. But I had made up my mind, and I believed the Lord was going to do great things. I often say we need to be more like the 90-year-old man who got married and started looking for a home in a good school district. We should always expect and believe God for great things. You see, before anything will ever be big in your life, it has to be big in your heart. And regardless of the odds, Rock Springs Church was big in my heart.

The Challenges Begin

When I became their new pastor, I was completely shocked to learn Rock Springs Church was around $5,000 in the red and had very little money coming in each week. They weren't able to pay the bills, which meant they weren't able to pay me much of a salary either. I was paid just $200 a week, and Barbara and I were also responsible for paying odd bills such as the phone line that ran from our house to the church. I guess that technically means Barbara was the first assistant at Rock Springs Church. We did have the little parsonage right on the church property to live in—an outdated ranch-style house. In our early days there, I had to sell furniture to supplement my income...I sold our living room suite and our bedroom suite just to make ends meet.

After only a few weeks of pastoring the church, I was working in the sanctuary one Thursday afternoon when a power truck pulled into the parking lot. When a worker climbed out, I asked him if there was a problem with our power. He responded, "Yes. Y'all are too far behind on the bill, so I'm here to cut you off." I couldn't believe what I was hearing—yet another financial burden.

I immediately thought there would be no way for us to have Sunday service if he cut the power off, so I asked him to please give me until Monday to get the money, thinking we could take up an offering on Sunday to help pay the past-due note. He agreed but promised to be back first thing Monday morning to either receive payment or cut the power.

When Sunday service arrived, I explained the urgency of the situation to our congregation, and the offering ended up being just enough to cover the bill.

That was the first time God had defied the odds for Rock Springs Church since I'd become their pastor, but He'd defied the odds there long before I arrived. In the early 1970s, the original, small, white church burned down, and the members decided to rebuild. A man named Roy Goggans was in charge of measuring and staking off exactly where the new building would stand. As he walked off the intended length of the church, he lost count of his steps and picked up with the last number he could remember. It turned out Roy overcounted his steps for the length of the building, and the church was built bigger than originally planned.

Many people said the building was bigger by mistake, but there are no mistakes when God is involved. He knew in advance that people would come to accept Christ and that the church would grow. Roy's "mistake" made just enough room for that growth.

More than anything, I was determined to see lives changed and salvations happen at Rock Springs Church, and when people get saved, they follow in believer's baptism. It was obvious that people had not been experiencing salvation and getting baptized because, upon further inspection of the baptistry, I found all the Christmas decorations stored in it. It had also somehow accumulated about two inches of mud on its floor—a clear sign that it had not been used in quite some time.

One Saturday morning, I grabbed a good scrub brush and two different cleaning products before heading to the church. After removing the Christmas decorations and scooping out the thick layer of old mud, I used Clorox and then Lysol to clean. With a Saturday's worth of work complete, the baptistry was up and running again, ready for new believers to follow in baptism.

When members of the congregation arrived for Sunday service the next morning, they got confused looks on their faces, wondering what the strange smell was in the sanctuary. I explained, "You smell a mixture of several cleaning supplies. I cleaned out the baptistry yesterday. People are going to get saved, and I'm going to baptize them!" The congregation may not have shared my optimism, but my confidence was in God because I knew what He could do. I expected Him to lead people to Rock Springs Church, where they would hear the gospel and get saved.

The average age of our congregation was somewhere between old enough to be my parents and old enough to be my grandparents. Barbara and I began to wonder where these people's children and grandchildren were. That thought was our starting point for inviting people to church. With a plan in place, we began knocking on doors, visiting with members of the community and inviting every family we met to church.

◆

Growth and Friction

Within the first year, we were averaging 99 people in attendance on Sunday mornings. The church was growing! But the difficulties and hurdles were growing just as quickly. Where there is motion, there's friction. Where there is opportunity, there's opposition. But I simply continued having big dreams for Rock Springs Church, and I expected God to do incredible things. I have always been convinced that we get what we expect, but the majority of people's "expector" has expired.

That seemed to be the case for the church board members at the time. They were hesitant to move forward with just about any new idea I presented, and they still wanted to vote on the type of vacuum cleaner to purchase for the church.

I had been pastoring the church for only eight months when several of the board members stated they didn't want me to have complete authority over who spoke and sang in Sunday services. They wanted to take a group vote each week to determine the songs for worship as well as what guest speakers I wanted to come to preach an evening service were acceptable. I argued that I could not pastor the church under those conditions. Debating every detail for the first eight months had been incredibly frustrating and stressful, and I was already exhausted.

A board meeting was held to make a final decision concerning whether I would have the authority over such decisions and the ability to pastor the church in a healthy way—without the board taking a vote over every detail. The probability of me continuing to pastor Rock Springs Church for much longer seemed pretty slim, but God used an unlikely person to defy the odds for my future.

Several of the men on the board who had supported me all along voted in favor of me having the necessary authority in decision-making while several other men on the board voted against it. The deciding vote came down to MaryAnne Niblett—the only woman to ever sit on the board at that time. MaryAnne had lived in Milner her entire life and had grown up in the church. She was the church treasurer and was greatly respected in the community. She had a lot to lose by supporting me.

Until this particular board meeting, MaryAnne had never spoken a word or made a motion. But she stood in that meeting and voted in favor of supporting my ability to make decisions. She had known me less than a year and had no way of being sure what kind of pastor I would become, but she trusted that God had sent me and chose to support me at such a critical time. I'm so thankful God used her in defying the difficult odds I faced my first year as pastor of Rock Springs Church.

With that obstacle behind me, I began deciding on necessary projects we needed due to the growth we were experiencing. Our first big one was paving a new parking lot that would replace the mostly dirt and minimal gravel lot used over the years. Paving the lot would cost $30,000, and I was determined to complete it debt-free. So we paved it one $4,000 section at a time. We raised the money through offerings, car washes, bake sales—you name it! Once we'd raised $4,000, a new section of the parking lot was paved, and then we went back to fundraising for the next section.

God provided every step of the way. If it's God's will, it's God's bill. Where God guides, He provides. Second Corinthians 9:8 says, "God will generously provide all you need. Then you will always have everything you need and plenty left over to share with others" (NLT). God wants to provide, but we must be determined in our kingdom work and willing to step out in faith, believing He can do abundantly more than "all that we ask or think" (Ephesians 3:20). After all, persistence is what got the snail on the ark!

It took a few years, but the entire parking lot was completed debt-free. But building space was also definitely needed because the church continued growing the entire time. During my second year there, Sunday school attendance had tripled in size. People throughout the community were coming, and many were accepting Christ for the first time. Lives were being changed, and the growth within the church was to be celebrated.

While my first few years at Rock Springs Church were incredibly difficult, I didn't let my circumstances drive me back to Tennessee. Trust me, there were times when Barbara and I both wanted to pack our bags. But every time we wanted to leave, we decided to stay. Many times over the years people in the church have disagreed with me and wanted us gone, but we stayed then too. I always figured that it would be much easier for them to move their membership than for me to move my furniture.

I don't believe anyone has ever accomplished greatness while also remaining comfortable. Success requires people to push past discomfort to make room for growth. The same is true in our walk with Christ—we achieve great things when we trust Him in uncomfortable situations and refuse to give up. Many times God will defy the odds in our lives once we're far outside of our comfort zone.

Moving outside of your comfort zone can be the easiest part of the process, but remaining in that uncomfortable place is the most challenging part. Maybe that time is now, when you've been obedient to God's calling yet you're wading through uncomfortable circumstances. But you can be persistent and have victory when you place great importance on three things: courage over comfort, calling over critics, and commitment over capability.

Courage over Comfort

The life that pleases God is often painful and difficult. Leaving a successfully growing church to pastor 30 people in the middle of nowhere was one of the hardest decisions I have ever made. Informing the supportive, loyal church members of Sweeton Hill Church that I was leaving was painful and difficult; so many of them had become like family to Barbara and me. We could have avoided the pain and chosen to remain comfortable while coasting through ministry, but the decision to be courageous over comfortable turned out to be a choice I would continue making throughout my ministry.

The same is true for your life as well. God will call you outside of your comfort zone to strengthen your faith for something more in the future. Joshua 1:5-6 details God's calling on Joshua's future. God said to him, "No man shall be able to stand before you all the days of your life. Just as I was with Moses, so I will be with you. I will not leave you or forsake you. Be strong and courageous, for you shall cause this people to inherit the land that I swore to their fathers to give them." God's calling on Joshua's life required him to trust the Lord for victory in every battle ahead.

Though circumstances will present seemingly impossible odds, remember that you serve a God of more. He's not interested in comfortable, content, or complacent. His plans require His people to be courageous, expectant, and hopeful. It takes courage to be persistent.

Calling over Critics

A.W. Tozer once said, "To be right with God has often meant to be in trouble with men."[1] Setting yourself apart will always set you up for criticism. If you want to call the shots, you must be willing to take the shots. People will offer their opinions whether or not you ask for them, and the Enemy will attack your thought life when you least expect it. Identifying the voice you're listening to is vitally important to remaining persistent in your walk with Christ.

People often doubt what they don't understand, and God's calling on your life may not make sense to others. But listening to the voices of criticism, whether from people's opinions or Satan's attacks, will leave you discouraged and doubtful. Those voices must be acknowledged and replaced, because the harder you pursue Christ, the louder the criticism will get.

John 6:63 gives a wonderful example of how God speaks to His people. Jesus said, "It is the Spirit who gives life; the flesh is no help at all. The words that I have spoken to you are spirit and life." Therefore, whatever thoughts or comments you hear throughout your day can be from God only if they are lifegiving and Spirit-filled. Don't mistake the lies of the Enemy, the flesh, or the critics for the Lord's voice of truth.

You will be able to clearly distinguish the voice of God only when you know it well, and that knowledge comes from regular studying and living out His Word. In Luke 11:28, Jesus said, "Blessed rather are those who hear the word of God and keep it!" Reading God's Word is powerful, but "keeping" His Word hidden in your heart and striving every day to become more like Jesus is how you become familiar with God's voice, which leads you to recognize it and trust it more. You can remain persistent in your walk with Christ when you allow His truth to drown out the critics.

Commitment over Capability

Have you ever found yourself at the start of an exciting, new opportunity only to become overwhelmed with unforeseen challenges that came rather quickly? The luster of possibility and potential can often blind you to the challenges that come with change. Whether new situations occur at work, within friendships, or at home, difficult challenges are certain to arise wherever people are involved. You'll find yourself facing circumstances you don't feel capable of handling, and you'll entertain the thought of bailing out.

Staying committed when you don't feel capable will position you to see God work in mighty ways. But let me be clear: There is a difference between difficult and dangerous circumstances. Putting yourself in harm's way is not the kind of commitment I'm talking about here. I'm talking about difficult circumstances that challenge you, stretch you, and require you to lean completely on the Lord. Those are the kinds of situations where commitment yields success.

Perhaps in your career a time will come when the excitement of promotion is quickly dulled by the stresses of the new position. Difficulties with colleagues, clients, and deadlines can leave you feeling as if you're drowning in responsibilities you don't seem capable of fulfilling.

Before you know it, you want to give up the position you worked so hard to secure.

The same can be true for marriages; the honeymoon phase often passes quicker than you hoped. Some people say marriage is made in heaven, but so are thunder and lightning. Often, marriages start as ideal but turn into an ordeal, and before long both people are looking for a new deal. Situations that leave you feeling incapable of moving forward will occur in any long-term relationship, and it will seem easier to start over with someone new than navigate the rough terrain of forgiveness and healing.

Let me hasten to say this: Anything easy to obtain in life is probably not worth having. Your greatest strengths will always be forged in the face of adversity. God can use you greatly once you surrender your capability to Him. In 2 Corinthians 12:9, Paul shared, "[The Lord] said to me, 'My grace is sufficient for you, for my power is made perfect in weakness.' Therefore I will boast all the more gladly of my weaknesses, so that the power of Christ may rest upon me."

When difficult circumstances arise, weakness should not bring embarrassment but encouragement. Cast all your cares on the One whose perfect power will deliver you from all you are incapable of facing on your own. After all, God never promised you a smooth flight, but He does promise you a safe landing. He will defy the odds in your life when you remain committed.

Adversity in life is inevitable, but persistence will always produce blessings. I often quote a poem by John Greenleaf Whittier titled "Don't Quit" as a way to motivate myself and others to remain persistent. Whittier ends his poem with these encouraging words: "So stick to the fight when you're hardest hit—It's when things seem worst that you must not quit."[2] Don't give up when difficulties arise. With God, you can overcome any obstacle. With God, you can defy all odds!

WELCOMING WEAKNESS

had many blessings to rejoice over in those first few years at Rock Springs Church. They were filled with miracle moments and tremendous church growth. But I also had some very low times in both my pastoral and personal life. While the church was prospering in many ways, the hits from the Enemy never quit coming in all areas.

Discrimination Raises Its Head

One low point came a year or so after I came to Rock Springs Church. I faced a situation that would define me not just as a pastor but as a person, and there would be a consequence to the stand I would take.

A white family in our church had been coming for quite some time when the man's sister became pregnant by a black man. The sister was hooked on drugs, and her little boy was placed with his family. They brought that precious and obviously multiracial little boy to church and other events, and a few members grew upset with their being "allowed" to do so.

One of the church leaders asked to meet with me privately to discuss the issue. During the meeting, he plainly said, "We don't want anyone bringing blacks to our church."

I immediately responded, "All people are welcome at Rock Springs Church. Jesus died for everyone."

He grew very angry at my answer and gave me an ultimatum. "I am a respected member of this church, and I give a lot of money each week. You're gonna have to make a decision. Either the black boy is leaving or I am."

Without hesitation, I said, "Well, I hate to see you go. We're gonna miss you."

He stormed out of my office that day and never came back to the church. His entire family, along with a few other families, moved their membership somewhere else. But even though he was a major contributor, I would never let anything matter more than loving and accepting all people. The consequence of those families leaving was not important. Rock Springs Church has always been and will always be a place for people of all races and from all walks of life.

While that situation was extremely difficult, it was a defining moment for me. My response to the situation made it clear to our congregation and to the community what kind of church Rock Springs would be—a church for all people.

Homesick

As hard hits were coming in my ministry, it seemed as if harder hits were coming in my personal life. Barbara and I grew so homesick that we had pretty much decided on returning home to Tennessee when the full year we'd committed to was up. But as usual, God had other plans for us, and He showed up at just the right time with just the right person.

One Sunday morning after a service, I stood at the door shaking hands with people as they left the sanctuary. An older woman named Norma Butler stayed longer than others to talk with me privately. Once everyone had left, she said, "Preacher Benny, you're going home, aren't you?"

I was shocked by her question—I had no idea how she knew what we were planning to do. But I will never forget what she said. "I can tell you're very homesick. You know, I live at the end of Rock Springs Road. You come on up there to my house, and I'll be your mama."

From that day forward, Norma Butler was our Georgia mama. She took care of us by providing dinner several nights a week and checking in on us regularly. She loved us like we were her children. She could see we were in a low place, and she chose to open her home to us and speak words of encouragement into our lives. God used her to deepen our roots in Georgia. If it hadn't been for Mrs. Norma's love and care, I'm not sure Barbara and I would have stayed. I'm so thankful she was faithful to listen and respond to God's prompting to care for us during such a weak time in our personal lives.

Battling Depression

While my homesickness subsided and I became happier with staying in Georgia, Barbara continued to struggle quite a bit. We had decided to stay past the first year, but darker times in our personal lives were heading our way. The odds of our staying at Rock Springs Church seemed to stack against us even higher in the year to come.

Barbara and I began trying to have children shortly after we were married. She was used to living in a house full of kids, and that's what we wanted for our home as well. All she had ever wanted was to be a mother, but after five years of marriage, that probability seemed to be growing slim. She was approaching 30 years old and was growing more concerned about not being able to have a baby.

Because of her past health problems, Barbara was worried there might be something wrong with her that prevented a pregnancy. We finally went to see a doctor to have tests run and procedures completed to determine a cause. After receiving the results, the doctor found no issues. I believe that hurt Barbara worse than if he had found a cause, because she lost all hope at that point.

One would assume church would be the best place for Barbara during this time, but it was probably the hardest place for her to be. Many women in the church were getting pregnant and inviting Barbara to their baby showers. Mother's Day services were the most painful for her to sit through, and people would often ask when we planned to grow our family. She would come to hear me preach at youth camps and interact with other people's children while worrying she may never see me interact with children of our own. What should have been a safe haven for her was actually a constant reminder of her inability to do the one thing she had ever wanted to do—have a baby.

Barbara grew depressed, and she went to bed and stayed there for six months. She lost 60 pounds and all desire to move forward with life. Our quiet and empty house taunted her inability to have children, so I took her to visit her family in Tennessee, where she could embrace the sounds of a lively family. Then I would pick her up to bring her back home, but once she walked inside, she'd say, "Take me back to Mama and Daddy's. I don't want to be here." It devastated me to see her that way, and I had no idea what I could do to make it better.

Barbara would stay with her parents for as long as a month and see her mother's doctor in Chattanooga, hoping for different conclusions about why she wasn't getting pregnant. New answers never came, and the depression forced her into even darker places.

Corrie ten Boom once said, "You can never learn that Christ is all you need until Christ is all you have."[1] And in our weakest moment, Christ was all we needed because He was all we had. There was no quick fix for our situation. I could do nothing in my own strength other than pray for God's guidance.

Later, through the help of a Christian psychologist, we realized Barbara associated our quiet home with the lack of feet "pitter-pattering" along the floors, what she longed to hear. But instead the silence was deafening, and depression was claiming more and more of her life.

Barbara's lowest point was the hardest day of my life. She stood under an old oak tree in our yard and said, "We want different things. You want this life down here in Georgia, and I want my life back in Tennessee. I don't want to be married to you anymore."

Nothing had ever hurt me as badly as those words hurt that day. But I knew it wasn't Barbara saying those things. Her depression made her feel and speak that way. Standing under that tree, I said, "Barbara, I don't believe that's you talking. I believe you're just depressed. I'll promise you this: If you still want to divorce me after you get on the other side of this depression, you can. But don't make such a major life decision right now." She agreed to wait, and I continued asking God to carry us through such a weak time.

Barbara doesn't remember having that conversation with me. In fact, she has no memory of ever saying many things she said during her battle. Depression has a way of stealing one's identity and replacing it with anger turned inward. No one should ever feel the need to apologize for being depressed or ever feel shame for what was said or done while battling depression. People suffering from depression are often taken to the darkest places in their minds and begin to believe the worst about themselves and others. They're not functioning as their true selves.

That Christian psychologist helped Barbara pinpoint the cause of her deep sadness and begin the process of getting well.

The Blessing of Adoption

Of course, Barbara still longed to be a mother, so we decided to begin the adoption process. Barbara immediately began feeling better, hopeful for the first time in almost a year. God was defying the odds in our personal life, and He was using all that had seemed so bad for so much good.

One night I was preaching at a church in Jackson, Mississippi, when Barbara called me in tears. Her mother had just been diagnosed with cancer. I told her how sorry I was to hear such terrible news and that I would rush straight home after finishing the service that night. I went back into the sanctuary, but not even 30 minutes passed before I received a second tap on the shoulder, informing me that another call had come through. When I picked up the phone, I heard Barbara crying again. She said, "Benny, Mama is dead."

I was shocked and confused by what I heard. We'd known her mother had been sick for a while and doctors had been treating her for everything under the sun, but by the time the doctors figured out it was cancer, the damage had been done. It was too late.

I was so worried that her mother's death would send Barbara back into depression, but her attitude concerning the situation was positive. She explained, "Had I not battled depression the way I did, I wouldn't have had all that time with Mama before she died. I had seven or eight wonderful months with her *because* of my depression." God used Barbara's weakest moments to give her quality time with her mother during her last days on earth.

God never wastes a hurt. He always takes what the devil means for bad and uses it for good. Again, Romans 8:28 says, "We know that God causes everything to work together for the good of those who love God and are called according to his purpose for them" (NLT). That's just what God did for Barbara. He took a time that seemed so dark and turned it into precious time well spent.

At the beginning of the adoption process, we learned the cost would be $8,000. We certainly didn't have that kind of money, and the odds of our being able to save enough by the time a baby was available seemed impossible. But once again we believed God for provision, and He used two wonderful, godly men to impact our lives in a great way.

The first man was a wonderful pastor named Ike Reighard. Pastor Ike came to speak at our church one Sunday and shared his heartbreaking testimony—he had lost both his unborn child and his wife during childbirth. Then at the end of the service, he asked the congregation to give ten times what they had planned toward the love offering for him because he wanted to give Barbara and me the money to help with our adoption cost. That night, the people gave $600 toward our adoption fund. What they didn't realize was that Ike's heart for adoption came from his own experience of adopting a child. God used difficult circumstances in Ike's life to burden his heart for others.

The second man God used was Howard Niblett, MaryAnne's husband. Upon hearing that we had begun the process of adoption, he made his first and only motion—for the church to help with the adoption of our child financially. Howard and MaryAnne cared deeply for us concerning adoption because they couldn't have children of their own either. Their burden for parents in the adoption process came out of their own painful experiences. God has a way of turning life's toughest battles into the greatest blessings.

The people of Rock Springs Church supported us through the entire process by continuing to give. By the time we finalized the adoption of our daughter, we had every bit of the $8,000. And more than supporting us financially, the people had prayed for and encouraged us through the difficult process of adoption. There were so many ups and downs along the way—so many unknowns we could not prepare for.

At the beginning, we had to answer many questions and provide every little detail about our lives to create a profile for birth parents to see when choosing an adoptive home for their baby. I found this to be incredibly stressful because I knew doctors and lawyers with profiles more appealing than ours were on the waiting list too. Yet even though we didn't have a lot of money or resources to provide for a child, we would most certainly provide as much love than anyone else. Maybe even more.

Savannah Abigail

A birth mother did choose us, and on August 9, 1993, we received a late-night call from the adoption agency letting us know our precious baby girl had been born. She would go to a temporary foster home for ten days while the birth mother decided whether to finalize the adoption. The agency also told us the baby had red hair, and they asked if we still wanted to adopt her. Apparently, some people had canceled adoptions because they thought red hair would make it more obvious that the child was adopted. I explained to the lady who called that we were beyond thrilled about her red hair because my mother was a redhead.

We were able to visit the little girl we named Savannah Abigail during the ten-day waiting period. I wanted to hold her so badly. I had never held a baby before, nor had I wanted to until that day. Savannah Abigail was the first and best baby to ever lie in my arms. Staring into her gorgeous blue eyes and seeing the red tint of what little hair she had, I realized a love I hadn't known before—the love a father has for his child.

Then when I saw Barbara holding Savannah, it was such a blessing to me. I've often said that I reaped the benefit of having Savannah, but Barbara deserved having her. The joy on my wife's face was more than

I could have ever hoped to see. I didn't think it was possible to love her any more than I already did until I saw her holding our daughter for the first time.

We prayed for those ten days to pass quickly so we could bring our baby girl home, but it was such a difficult time as we tried so hard to stay positive. We were all too aware that the birth mother could change her mind. But when the ten-day waiting period came to an end, we received a call letting us know it was time to bring our baby girl home. Barbara was on cloud nine, and Savannah Abigail's arrival made our house a home. We were beyond excited about what God had done for us and how He had made a way for us to have a family of our own.

When Savannah was six years old, she began asking questions about God and expressing her desire for salvation. I had the incredible privilege of leading Savannah to Christ one night in our home. I always tell parents not to pressure their children when it comes to accepting Jesus. Just teach them Scripture and let God work in their hearts. And I encourage parents to not miss out on the blessing of leading their own child to faith in Christ.

I remember telling Savannah Abigail how proud I was of her. I explained that because she was our adopted daughter, we couldn't be at the hospital for her physical birth, but we were so proud to be present for her spiritual birth. And if I had been given the choice between the two, I would have chosen her spiritual birth. It was one of the greatest moments in my life.

Over the years Barbara and I found ourselves in seasons of tremendous weakness, but we continued to believe God for big things. We believed Jeremiah 29:11: "I know the plans I have for you, declares the LORD, plans for welfare and not for evil, to give you a future and a hope." God's promises are good, and His plans are perfect. He has always been faithful to show up in our weakest moments with perfect timing and provision.

Again, in 2 Corinthians 12:9 Paul says of Jesus, "He said to me, 'My grace is sufficient for you, for my power is made perfect in weakness.' Therefore I will boast all the more gladly of my weaknesses, so that the power of Christ may rest upon me." This is another one of those verses that's easy to say but hard to live. Most people's first instinct isn't to welcome weakness with boasting and gladness. Our flesh often tells us the opposite—to be ashamed of any weakness. We don't see weakness the way God sees it.

People see weakness as an obstacle while God sees opportunity. We see a problem, but He sees potential. We see brokenness, but He sees benefit. People think weakness is a setback, but God knows it's a setup. After all, our faith is built on what seemed to be Christ's weakest moment but was in fact God's power at work to bring about salvation for all mankind.

The very same power that raised Jesus from the grave is at work in your life, and God wants you to see your weaknesses as opportunities. If you want to experience His resurrecting power and see Him defy the odds in your life, you must understand how weakness restrains pride, requires the Holy Spirit, and reveals purpose.

Weakness Restrains Pride

When life is flowing smoothly and successes begin to stack up, it can be easy to believe we're the one making good things happen. We're putting in the hard work, and the rewards are rolling in as they should. We pat ourselves on the back and graciously receive accolades from those around us. But let me hasten to say that anything that isn't turned into praise will turn into pride.

Allowing yourself to believe you have accomplished anything on your own will permit pride to begin a slow swell in your heart. In 1 Peter 5:5, the Bible teaches that "God opposes the proud but gives grace to the humble." Verses 6 and 7 then explain the benefits of humility: "Humble yourselves, therefore, under the mighty hand of God so that at the proper time he may exalt you, casting all your anxieties on him, because he cares for you." Pride will render you incapable of fulfilling God's calling on your life, but welcoming weakness will restrain pride.

God wants to exalt you and use your life to accomplish great and mighty things for His kingdom, but you must acknowledge your weaknesses and understand that you have no power apart from Him. The Bible compares our purest actions to dirty rags because we are all sinners and fall short of the glory of God. We all have weaknesses and walk through difficult seasons that leave us powerless.

Only obedience in weakness, whether in moments or in seasons, will result in your fully knowing God's strength. He wants you to cast all your worries and imperfections on Him alone. When you realize that weakness restrains pride and humility places you back under His mighty hand, you will boast gladly of your weakness, knowing that God will provide you with strength like only He can.

Weakness Requires the Holy Spirit

Weak moments will leave you wondering what to do, where to go, and what to pray. Weakness has a way of causing you to question your calling and purpose. God, in His sovereignty, knew you would need the Holy Spirit to guide you through the ups and downs of daily life and give you power in difficult circumstances. Before Jesus went to the cross, He told His disciples that He would send a "helper" who would give them power. That helper is the Holy Spirit.

In Romans 8:26, Paul wrote, "The Spirit helps us in our weakness. For we do not know what to pray for as we ought, but the Spirit himself intercedes for us with groanings too deep for words." Therefore, weakness is a magnet for the Holy Spirit, and He pleads with God on your behalf. Denying weakness not only keeps you from seeking God's strength but keeps you from experiencing the fullness of the Holy Spirit in your life.

When you feel as though you're drowning in life's troubles, too weak to keep your head above water, the Holy Spirit is pleading with God to provide you with His sustaining strength. The Holy Spirit prays for God to give you the right answer, the next step, and the proper provision to move forward despite your weakness.

Understanding how the Holy Spirit responds in weak moments allows you to see why Paul was boasting gladly about his weaknesses. He wasn't happy about the hardships he was facing, but he rejoiced in knowing how close the Holy Spirit was in his weakest state. He knew his weakness required the Holy Spirit to move in his life; therefore, he welcomed his weaknesses in order to experience the fullness and power of the Holy Spirit.

Weakness Reveals Purpose

Weaknesses in your life may not immediately appear to be opportunities, but God will use your weakest moments to equip you for a unique purpose. Surrendering your weaknesses to God will develop a deeper trust in Him through difficult times as well as develop empathy and compassion in your heart for others who may share the same struggles.

I've come to realize that I minister more out of my pain than out of my success. My highlighted weaknesses have allowed me to connect with others countless times. Instead of being ashamed of my struggles, I surrendered them before the Lord to draw others to Him.

You see, we often look at those around us as having it all together while believing we are the only ones struggling. But in reality, way more connects us than separates us. When we allow the walls of shame to come down and we share our struggles, God can minister through us to bring healing to so many others.

Second Corinthians 1:3-4 says, "Blessed be the God and Father of our Lord Jesus Christ, the Father of mercies and God of all comfort, who comforts us in all our affliction, so that we may be able to comfort those who are in any affliction, with the comfort with which we ourselves are comforted by God." These verses show how God not only comes to your rescue but uses everything you experience—good and bad—to prepare you for the unique purpose of ministering to others at just the right time. Nothing at all happens by accident—God has a purpose in and for all of the struggles you face.

This world will not hesitate to provide you with your fair share of difficulty. Hard times will come and weaknesses will leave you feeling defeated. After all, in John 16:33 Jesus told His disciples, "Here on earth you will have many trials and sorrows" (NLT). But I'm so thankful that He didn't stop there. Jesus went on to say, "But take heart, because I have overcome the world." You will most likely experience more tough days than tremendous days because difficulty will remind you to rely solely on God.

I'm so glad to report that we do not serve a God who is distant and disconnected from our struggles. Hebrews 4:15-16 says, "We do not have a high priest who is unable to sympathize with our weaknesses, but one who in every respect has been tempted as we are, yet without sin. Let us then with confidence draw near to the throne of grace, that we may receive mercy and find grace to help in time of need." In fact, we serve a God who knows us intimately and understands the heartache we often feel. So don't let weaknesses distance you from God; instead, allow them to direct you to the feet of Jesus.

Welcoming weaknesses will create a dependence on the Lord, and then you'll experience His power like never before. God will use your point of greatest weakness to defy the odds in your life and impact the lives of those around you.

LIFE IS A MARATHON, NOT A SPRINT

ncredibly detail-oriented people are often criticized with this old idiom: "You can't see the forest for the trees." While I understand the common expression, I've never been able to relate to it. Before coming to know the Lord, I wasn't much worried about the forest or the trees, but since salvation, I've always seen the forest and figured God will worry about the trees. I'm a big-picture person who focuses on what can happen when God is involved. My attitude has always been *Don't tell me about the labor pains; show me the baby!* A good leader's job is to cast vision, and the end goal has always been my focus. So I don't get blinded by details.

To encourage my staff to visualize their dreams and goals in life and in ministry, I often share these words from my good friend Pastor Johnny Hunt: "If you don't see it before you see it, you'll never see it."

In the early years of Rock Springs Church, most people stepped onto the property only to see a small brick chapel with a white awning covering the front steps that led to a tiny sanctuary with unfinished spaces. But each time I stepped foot on that property, I saw a forest and believed God would worry about the trees.

I saw hundreds of people in attendance, buses picking up children for church, a family life center full of activity, and a church campus sprawling with ministries to serve the wonderful people living in and around our community. God gave me a vision for Rock Springs Church, and I've spent my life since then allowing Him to use me in making it a reality. I knew just as He had defied the odds in growing my family, He had great plans to do the same with Rock Springs Church. So I began attending conferences and meeting with pastors to gain wisdom from their experiences and mistakes.

For several months Barbara and I saved money to attend our first Elmer Towns conference on church growth. Mr. Towns had written a book titled *154 Steps to Revitalize Your Sunday School and Keep Your Church Growing*. One big idea I took away from the conference was Friend Day—a Sunday where each church member invited one unchurched friend to attend the service and other festivities. Hosting a Friend Day at Rock Springs Church seemed like the perfect way to reach people in our community.

After returning home, we began making preparations to host our very first Friend Day. The goal was to have 300 people in attendance, and as an incentive, I promised to swallow a live goldfish during the service if we reached that goal. Some people might think I'm a nut, but I'm screwed onto the right bolt! I wasn't trying to get people to attend so I could have a good count; I tried to get people to attend because people count.

On June 2, 1996, more than 300 people attended our "Fishing for Jesus Day." And yes, I swallowed a live goldfish at the end of the service. Of course, if I did something like that in a service today, I would have animal rights activists protesting on the church steps. It may seem like a silly gimmick to get people to church, but I've always said, "I'm for a dog…if he'll bark for Jesus!" If swallowing a goldfish or taking a pie to the face will get nonbelievers to church, sign me up.

A Goal for Growth

As our church grew, I decided to attend a John Maxwell conference called Challenge 1,000. John Maxwell, along with other speakers such as Andy Stanley, spoke to an audience of pastors about leadership and church growth. At the end of the conference, John Maxwell led a special prayer over pastors who believed they were called to build a church of 1,000 plus.

The invitation was given, and I felt God nudge me to go down for prayer. He said I was called to build Rock Springs Church to more than a thousand members. As I stepped into the aisle, the pastors I went to the conference with began to laugh and whisper. Satan wanted me to return to my seat because he knew God was up to something big. I would be lying if I said the laughter didn't hurt; I had battled insecurity all my life, so Satan knew just where to attack. I'm sure those guys looked at our little church in Milner, Georgia, and saw impossible odds. How could a church our size ever have a membership of 1,000, let alone more? What they didn't seem to realize was that I served an odds-defying God who, again, "is able to do far more abundantly than all that we ask or think" (Ephesians 3:20).

I left that conference with a clear vision and a new contact. Pastor Bill Purvis of Cascade Hills Church in Columbus, Georgia, had spoken at the conference, and I decided to reach out to him for a meeting. While spending a day with him at Cascade Hills, he encouraged me in my calling to build a church of 1,000 members, and he expressed his interest in helping me in any way he could. He asked if I had been recording my sermons in order to sell cassette tapes, but I told him we didn't have the resources to purchase that kind of equipment. Bill sent me home with a wealth of knowledge and a duplicator that would allow me to record my sermons and sell them to raise money toward a building program. The encouragement he gave me that day meant so much more to me than the duplicator.

God used Bill Purvis to not only encourage me in growing Rock Springs Church but also to develop a passion in me for helping other pastors. My experiences with receiving help and encouragement from other local pastors had been quite negative up until this point. Once I wanted to print 30 bulletins for a Sunday service, and I asked a local church if I could purchase the materials and then run my bulletins on their machine. The pastor responded, "I'll let you do it this time, but don't come back." No other pastors in my area seemed to have any desire to see my ministry succeed. Therefore, Bill's support was monumental to me.

Making Room for Growth

With the duplicator I received from Bill, we began recording sermons and selling them in the foyer of the church. All proceeds from the tapes were put into a building fund for a multipurpose facility—a family life center that would provide additional Sunday school space, a fellowship hall, and a gym for youth activities. God told me to build the new facility debt-free—a much bigger step in faith than paving the parking lot—plus it would take $300,000 to complete it.

We decided to raise $100,000 before breaking ground and then raise the additional funds as the construction progressed. The chances of completing the facility debt-free may have seemed unlikely, but God's work done God's way never lacks God's support. We just started raising money every way we could and trusted Him to provide.

The Alvis Butler Family Life Center, as it would be called, would be a 100-square-foot facility built with no architect and no professional plans. The plans were sketched on a piece of notebook paper during a board meeting as we discussed and decided on the desired layout. But while we thought we knew the most efficient design for the building, God had different plans in mind.

As construction on the building progressed, God began to move providentially. Just before finalizing the roof structure for the building, a member of the board casually mentioned that raising the height of the roof by one to two feet would allow for a second-floor addition in the future if it were ever needed. While many people couldn't imagine ever needing that much space for our small congregation, we decided to increase the height of the roof. What seemed like a simple suggestion was in fact God's provision for the incredible growth Rock Springs Church would experience within the next few years.

Fundraising and donations had been quite successful throughout the construction, but nearing the end of the project, the church lacked the final $10,000 it would take to pay in full. All fundraising options had been exhausted and new donations were few and far between. We had made it to $290,000 debt-free, and I just couldn't imagine having to borrow the remaining amount.

The builder called me one Thursday afternoon to say he needed to receive the remaining $10,000 in order to complete the finishing touches and pay his employees, and I asked him to give me until Monday morning. I had no idea what difference the weekend would make—the Sunday offering certainly wouldn't cover the bill—but that afternoon I sat at my little desk in the basement of our little sanctuary and prayed. *God,* I said, *You told me to build this facility debt-free. You have provided every step of the way, and I know You will see this through. I just give this all to You.*

As I sat at my desk again the next morning, preparing for the Sunday service, I received a phone call from a lawyer's office. He informed me that a man who wasn't a member of our church had died and Rock Springs Church was a beneficiary of his estate. I was quite shocked by what the man was saying, because I didn't even know the deceased individual, and he didn't seem to have any connection to our church. The lawyer said a check would be sent immediately.

Not being able to contain my curiosity, I said, "Do you mind letting me know the amount left to the church?"

"I don't mind at all. It's $10,000."

Upon ending that call, I began praising God right there in my little office. I knew He had provided that money for the building in His perfect timing through a way only He could receive all the credit. On April 26, 1998, the Alvis Butler Family Life Center was dedicated with a record attendance of 501, and God certainly received the glory, honor, and praise for all He had done.

I'm not one to believe in luck or coincidence but only in the providential hand of God. Someone once showed me a rabbit's foot and asked if I knew what it meant. I responded, "Yeah. It means a rabbit is running around somewhere with only three feet." But when I've told the story of that $10,000 check over the years, people have tried to explain how common it is for people to leave money to a church. But nothing of the sort had ever been done in the history of our church, nor has it been done since. There's no explaining how it happened outside of God's good hand upon Rock Springs Church.

God used that situation to build my faith and once again show me He could defy all odds. Ecclesiastes 11:4 says, "Farmers who wait for perfect weather never plant. If they watch every cloud, they never harvest" (NLT). There's no perfect timing outside of God's timing. If you wait until you have enough money to get married, you'll never get married. If you wait until you have enough money to have children, you'll never have children. And if we had waited until we had enough money to build the Butler Building, it never would have happened. God just wants us to step out in faith, trusting that He'll provide.

A Shocking Truth Revealed

During this time of exciting growth in our church, God was also working behind the scenes in my own life. I was 30 years old when God continued defying the odds concerning one of my deepest hurts—one I rarely shared with anyone.

As an adult, I had come to terms with growing up without a father. It came as a complete surprise, then, when Rhonda informed me that Lee Tate was not our biological father as I had believed my whole life. But I wasn't comfortable talking to Mama about the details of how I came to be, so I avoided the topic and buried my emotions along with my questions.

Then Rhonda did some research to find her biological father, and she wanted to help me find mine too. After doing a good bit of digging, we discovered my biological father's name was Don Wisdom, his first name the same as my stepfather's had been. Once Rhonda had his name, it wasn't hard to find contact information for him. In true Rhonda fashion, she called and said he needed to get in touch with me and meet me in person. But he had no intentions of doing that. He had a family of his own when he met and spent a night with my mother, and that's why he made a point of not being a part of my life—it would have ruined the life he already had.

With little consideration for his circumstances, Rhonda gave him an ultimatum: "Call Benny tomorrow at noon or I will call your wife to inform her of your secret." He had no choice but to call me the very next day. I'm not sure if I had ever been so nervous to answer a call.

Don and I talked for an hour or so before deciding to meet the next day at a Shoney's in Nashville. I made the five-hour drive north with so much apprehension. I didn't know what he would look like. I didn't know the proper questions to ask him. I had no idea what to expect. All I knew was that I would be meeting my father for the very first time, and I was so nervous.

As I walked into that restaurant and laid eyes on Don, I felt relieved to finally put a face to the shadow I had longed to come to light ever since I learned Lee Tate wasn't my biological father. I introduced myself and shook his hand, and I was overwhelmed with many different emotions. Over lunch, I listened to him tell me about his wife and five children, his jobs throughout the years, and the many mistakes he made along the way.

Our conversation lasted for several hours, and much to my surprise, he already knew a lot about me because he'd kept up with my life over the years. He came to hear me preach several times, and he had even bought my sermon tapes. At the time, I couldn't process how that made me feel. He'd been a spectator of my life, and I never even knew it.

To say that my emotions toward him were all positive and optimistic would be a lie because anger built up in me as I sat through that first meeting with him. It hurt me deeply to hear him talk about his other children. I was mad that I had always been and would continue to be a secret from his "real" family. He wanted any future meetings to be away from his home and for us to make contact only through his business phone and address. The meeting I had hoped would bring healing brought only more hurt.

All my life I had wondered what it would be like to have a father. As a young child, I would hide in a closet and whisper "Daddy" just to know what it sounded like coming out of my mouth. Now all I had longed for was sitting in front of me in a Shoney's. But I knew I could choose to either dwell on the past and what I didn't have all those years or focus on the possibility of building some sort of relationship with my father in the years to come.

I chose the latter because forgiveness and acceptance are two things Jesus's life on earth exemplified. His entire purpose was to offer forgiveness for our sins through His death on the cross. Romans 5:8 reminds us that "God showed his great love for us by sending Christ to die for us while we were still sinners" (NLT). If God accepts me as I am and offers me forgiveness, I should strive to do the same for others. I chose to offer forgiveness to my father with the hope of a better future.

Yet a future with Don would be much shorter than I anticipated. Before I headed back to Georgia, he told me he was on dialysis. The same day I met my biological father for the first time was the same day he told me he was dying. He had been on dialysis for some time, and he had only a few more years to live. I asked if he had ever experienced salvation, and much to my relief, Don had accepted Christ two years ago. He'd made his way to a little church and given his life to the Lord.

Don made sure I knew how sorry he was for everything that happened with my mother. He said he knew she was a good person and he was to blame for taking advantage of her at a young age. But he went on to say, "What your mom and I meant for evil, God meant for good." God had taken their sinful situation and used it for His glory.

I knew Don was struggling with feelings of regret, because he said, "I hate what I've done. We've spent no time together, but because I gave my life to Christ, maybe we can spend eternity together." He was absolutely right; while we had only five years together on this earth, we have eternity together in heaven.

I hadn't known if there would be closure for me concerning my biological father on this side of heaven, but God was so good to give me time with Don before his passing. Even after Don died, God continued to move in a mighty way through uniting me with half-siblings I had never known. Don's five children learned about me after he died. The news was hurtful, but as time passed, they decided to reach out. They were eager to know all about me, and I felt the same way about them.

When we met, we talked for quite some time and then decided we would like to stay in touch. Over the years, I was able to build strong relationships with three of them. God also gave me the sweetest blessing of being able to lead two of my brothers to Christ.

My young life may have been filled with hardships and lacked family support, but God has given me eternity with my family through Jesus Christ. I'm so grateful for how He has used every bad thing in my life for my good and His glory. He has restored my life and my heart in ways I never thought possible, and situations I deemed irreparable have been redeemed through God's goodness. The Lord protected my family, led us to salvation in Jesus, healed my wife, and brought closure to deep insecurities.

And then just when I think He's done it all, God shows up and does more.

Hindsight is always 20/20. It's easy to look back and clearly see how specific pieces came together to create the intricate picture God has been faithfully working on. The difficulty lies in being patient when His time line doesn't match ours.

In John 11, Mary and Martha send for Jesus because they believe He will heal their brother. But Jesus waits two days, and Lazarus dies before Jesus comes and raises him from the dead. I'm sure the sisters were confused as to why Jesus was waiting so long. If He loved Lazarus so much, why didn't He come right away to heal him?

We often ask ourselves a similar question when we're facing difficult circumstances: *If God loves me so much, why is He letting these things happen, and why is it taking Him so long to show up?* While we see our immediate circumstances and want a quick healing, God sees the bigger picture and wants a resurrection, because when He blesses us, He has more than us in mind.

God didn't create an explosion in the membership of Rock Springs Church overnight, and He didn't provide a father when I first began asking for one. Instead, He defied the odds through day-to-day choices and used different people and situations as intricate parts of a story only He could write. While our desire for answers is tied to emotion, His purpose is always tied to eternity.

God doesn't always move when or how we believe He should, but

He always moves with perfect precision and provision. We must be careful to remember that this life we've been given is a marathon, not a sprint. God can defy the odds when we yield to His timetable. We will see Him move in mighty ways, but only when we're willing to wait, willing to work, and willing to worship.

Willing to Wait

Because of incredible advancements in technology, we're living in a world where things are readily available to us at any moment. With same-day shipping and food delivery apps, we never have to wait long for much of anything. But as wait times have shortened, so has our patience.

We often want God to move as quickly as our Amazon order does, but His response time doesn't always line up with our expectations. What we believe to be unanswered prayers can leave us sitting with our arms crossed, pouting over our circumstances. But God wants us to wait patiently and trust in His perfect timing instead of running ahead of or withdrawing from Him.

Habakkuk 2:3 says, "The vision awaits its appointed time; it hastens to the end—it will not lie. If it seems slow, wait for it; it will surely come; it will not delay." Habakkuk looked around at all the terrible things going on in the world and grew angry. God's response to his questions and complaints required Habakkuk to wait patiently. Just because answers are slow to arrive doesn't mean they're late. God promises that His plans are never delayed.

You may look around at all the evil and injustice in the world today and wonder why God is allowing such tragedy. You may have questions and complaints about life's difficulties just like Habakkuk did. But God's response has not changed. He says to wait patiently. Be willing to wait on His perfect provision; it will always show up at just the right time. Don't give up on believing in God for big things. In time, He will provide answers and healing to situations you may have declared too far gone. Hold tight to the truth and remember "it will surely come."

Willing to Work

Although God wants us to wait patiently, He doesn't want us to wait passively. In the same way athletes don't sit idle through the off-season waiting for their first game, Christians should not grow lazy in seasons of waiting. The requirement to wait does not mean retirement from work. We must be willing to work diligently right where God has us regardless of not knowing the answers to all of our questions.

I have often stressed to my staff and congregation that a willingness to work is vitally important. I truly believe that nothing will work in your life until you do. My mother instilled a strong work ethic in Rhonda and me. I can remember her saying things like, "If you want to rise to the top, you've gotta get off your bottom," and "If you want your pockets to jingle, you gotta shake a leg!" I've always believed that successful people are the ones who are willing to work.

An average person may be able to get up from their couch and sprint to the mailbox and back on any given day, but it takes months of practice and preparation to run a marathon. The same is true for our Christian walk. We may not see how God is working in our lives for months or even years, but we must diligently strive to know Him daily if we are to endure the hardships that will come along the way.

Although our circumstances may be ever-changing, our purpose in life always remains the same: Know God and make Him known. While easy to say and easy to read, both are extremely hard to do when so much constantly competes for our attention. It takes discipline and preparation to pursue Christ every day. But instead of focusing on learning the answers to all of our questions, we must work hard to know the One who has all the answers.

First Peter 3:15 says, "In your hearts honor Christ the Lord as holy, always being prepared to make a defense to anyone who asks you for a reason for the hope that is in you; yet do it with gentleness and respect." This Scripture exemplifies our purpose perfectly. When we work hard to know Christ, others can't help but notice a difference in our actions and attitudes. We then have an opportunity to share the gospel with those who don't know Jesus. Even though we don't have all the answers to what's going on in and around our lives, we can continue living out our purpose and work to become all God created us to be. He is faithful to work in the waiting, and we should do the same.

Willing to Worship

God never guaranteed this life would be easy. In fact, as I mentioned before, He promises the exact opposite. And again, in John 16:33, Jesus said to His disciples, "In the world you will have tribulation. But take heart; I have overcome the world." The promise of victory is so encouraging, but the tribulation is still tough to endure. If we are to run the race with endurance—to succeed in the marathon of life—we must cling to the promises of God and lift our hands in praise.

Worshipping God through difficulty forces us to focus on our Savior instead of on our challenging situation. We must refuse to be consumed with all of the unknowns and remember to celebrate all that God has already done in our lives. Power is released through praise, and knowing the answers to our questions does us no good if God's power isn't present in our difficulties.

Be willing to worship God even when nothing seems to be happening. Why? Because He has already done enough. If God never does another thing for us, He has already done more than we deserve. Worship will change our attitude, invite His presence into our lives, and pave the way for miracles, but we must be willing to worship Him despite our circumstances.

I could have grown tired of the difficult daily tasks of building the church God called me to build, and I could have grown bitter toward Him concerning a relationship with my biological father. My emotions fought for control on so many tough days. But I continued to believe God for the *what* instead of the *when*.

Remaining patient when answers are few and far between is challenging, and working hard when nothing seems to be happening can be incredibly draining. Worshipping God when the future seems so unclear may be the last thing you want to do. But I can promise you that God always rewards obedience, and His hand of blessing is on those who purpose in their heart to know Him and make Him known.

God builds little by little, and it will take faith plus patience to see Him move in your life in mighty ways. You may not always have the answers when you want them, but you will be able to look back and see evidence of God's hand in everything you have ever done. I know beyond the shadow of a doubt that God can defy the odds in your life when you yield to His timetable and remember that life is a marathon, not a sprint.

EMBRACE CHANGE

By fall of 2000, Rock Springs Church was growing so rapidly that we began discussing plans to take advantage of that last-minute opportunity to add a second floor to the Butler building. Sunday school rooms were filling quickly, and it was becoming impossible to find an empty seat in the 11:00 a.m. service. While the obvious next step was to add an earlier service, there was inevitable opposition to that idea.

Several older members of the congregation believed starting a second service would divide the church. But while they saw division, God saw addition. I knew Rock Springs Church would never grow to all God wanted it to be if we were too afraid to change. When the first Sunday arrived with the newly added 8:30 a.m. service, only 25 people attended. But the number continued to grow each week, and despite the concerns of our older crowd, attendees of both services continued coming together in Sunday school classes and fellowship activities. The church was one—a rapidly growing one.

By 2002, the second floor of the Butler Building had been completed for additional Sunday school space and a youth room. The balcony in the sanctuary was completed for additional space as well, and every building on the church campus was bursting at the seams for both services! God continued to provide by sending us people to serve and lead in many capacities. A wonderful couple began leading worship and greatly impacted our services by taking worship to a new level. God also sent a new youth pastor to lead and grow our youth ministry in an incredible way.

Church attendance and membership growth were on the rise. People were getting saved, following in baptism, and joining the church. God was moving, and we were out of room. We did the very best we could to create additional space, placing chairs throughout the sanctuary. But the crowd eventually overflowed into the foyer and even onto the front porch. With the doors flung wide open, people sat in folding chairs under the awning out there just to hear the service. The proposal of a new sanctuary should have been a no-brainer, and God was calling me to the biggest leap of faith yet.

A $4,000,000 Miracle

I scheduled a meeting with the board and had plans drawn up for a new sanctuary. The proposal included a 1,200-seat, auditorium-style sanctuary with a $4,000,000 price tag. It's safe to say the board was scared to death. Their immediate response? "No way can we afford a building like that." I told them we had only two options: build a new sanctuary or put *Go to hell, we're full!* on our marquee.

They understood the need for the building, but the odds seemed too high to fill a sanctuary that size much less be able to pay for it. I explained, "I know a project this size scares you to death, but not following God's will scares me more."

By the time that board meeting ended, we had committed to building the new sanctuary. But the weight of the decision to move forward on such an enormous project didn't fully hit me until I was sitting in my car. A wave of stress and anxiety began to crash down on me, and the confidence I had in the meeting disappeared in the silence. I couldn't help but pray, *God, what have I gotten us into? There's no way I can do this. I need You more than ever.*

I may have had the support of the board, but it seemed impossible that I would ever find a bank to support our plans. Bank after bank turned me down when they saw the new building's price tag for a church our size in a town so small. One bank executive said, "You don't have the clientele to pay for a building this size." But I wasn't taking no for an answer, so the search continued until I found a bank that agreed to a $4,000,000 loan to be paid off over the course of 30 years. The numbers were terrifying, but I held to the one truth that gave me all the confidence to move forward—God was in control.

With construction underway on the new sanctuary, we continued doing everything we could to raise money to meet the loan payments. The same year we broke ground, I wrote my first book, *One More Night with the Frogs*. It was a million "cellar," because Barbara often tells me we have a million copies down in the cellar. I wrote my second book, *Happy Wife, Happy Life*, the very next year, and all proceeds from its sales went toward the building fund. We continued to have "chicken-ques," sell sermon series CDs, and host a variety of other fundraising events. I was determined to prove those banks wrong about Rock Springs Church.

Regardless of the hard work from pastors and members, we had obstacles throughout the build at every turn. I always say, "When God gets to blessin', the devil gets to messin'." And the devil created two huge messes that caused the odds to stack against the success of the new sanctuary. They both put incredible financial strain on what was already an overwhelming step in faith.

As the construction crew neared the point of installing the roof, the metal for it hadn't yet arrived on site. Still, with assurance that it was in transport and would be delivered within a few days, the sheetrock crew began work on the walls inside. The "few days" passed, and the weather report said rain was heading our way. Upon further investigation of the metal's whereabouts, we were informed that the order hadn't yet been placed and the metal was not on the way. The rain moved in and ruined the newly hung drywall throughout the building, requiring the purchase of thousands of dollars of replacement materials. With obstacles of that kind popping up, the stress over finances continued to grow.

When construction was coming to an end, moving into the new sanctuary was becoming a reality. Excitement was high and the stress of the build was easing. Barbara and I visited the sanctuary one evening to walk through and take in all that had been accomplished. We were in awe of the size and beauty of the new sanctuary. We walked over to the little chapel and began praying over the pews as we had done each week. I knelt to pray and told God, "I don't know how I'm ever going to pay for that building, and I don't know how I'll ever fill all of those seats." I immediately heard Him respond as loud and clear as ever, *You didn't fill the sanctuary you're in now.*

God's response humbled me, but it also gave me so much confidence that the weight of the growth at Rock Springs Church was God's alone. He was so faithful to continue building my faith through every trial I faced, and He will do the same in your life. God will use every trial to build your faith and your relationship with Him. Even if you begin to doubt or stress out when the odds are stacked against you, He will remind you of His power and presence. He will show you grace in times of weakness.

The Old Testament provides many examples of how the Israelites continued to doubt God after He rescued them from slavery in Egypt. It can be easy to judge them for how frequently they questioned God's provision, but the same can be true for us as we let doubt and anxiety creep in when the odds against us are stacked high and a situation becomes stressful. But just as God did with the Israelites, He always reminds us of His power and gives us a new opportunity to exhibit faith. Daily praising God and remembering His perfect track record of faithfulness can serve as preparation for battles ahead.

God's Encouraging Message

With construction on the new sanctuary finished, August 15, 2004, was dedication Sunday—a celebration of all God had done. Much to everyone's surprise, the sanctuary was full. Average attendance had reached almost 950 by the end of the year, and everyone was in awe of what God had accomplished. It was such an exciting time for Rock Springs Church, but while we continued to celebrate, praise, and give thanks, Satan got to work on the biggest obstacle yet.

After we'd been in the new sanctuary for a few short weeks, my assistant told me several men had requested counseling appointments with me. But after the first meeting, I quickly realized they weren't seeking counseling; they were seeking payment. Subcontractors were coming to my office demanding payment for the work they'd done on our new building. Although I'd made all of the final payments to the contractor, they had not been paid.

Come to find out, the final $400,000 I paid to the contractor never made its way to his subs, and now hardworking men were coming to the church and calling my house wanting to know what I intended to do about it. But I could do nothing—all financial resources were exhausted and money coming in designated for the sanctuary had to go toward the loan payments.

This was the most difficult situation I had ever experienced in my entire life. All I could do was ask God for guidance. I was so stressed that I couldn't even get one good night of sleep. Waking up at 1:00 a.m. became my new normal for several months, and many times I would head to the little community park near my house to walk its track and pray. I was always the only one at the park at that hour, but one of those early morning prayer walks included a miraculous experience I will remember for the rest of my life.

As I walked along the track asking God for wisdom and guidance in the situation, I saw a woman walking ahead of me. I hadn't seen her walk onto the track, and I had no clue where she came from. She walked ahead of me for just a moment before stopping to turn toward me and ask, "Are you a preacher?"

The answer that ran through my mind in the moment was *I don't want to be right now*. But when I finally said I was, she looked at me intently and said, "You're going through a difficult time. You trust God, you place it all in His hands, and He'll work it out."

I immediately dropped my head and started crying. Her comment had caught me by surprise, and I couldn't contain my emotion. After only a few seconds, I raised my head to look at the woman, but she was no longer there. I looked in every direction around the park, but she was nowhere to be found. I had never seen her before, and I have never seen her since that early morning. Hebrews 13:2 says some have "entertained angels without realizing it!" (NLT). To this day, I believe that woman was an angelic being God sent to encourage my heart and say *Trust Me. I can defy the odds.*

While that divine encounter was truly an amazing experience, God had only shown me a small portion of the miracles He was preparing to perform. At the time, only two people knew anything about the financial conundrum we were being dragged through—the chairman of the board and me. I had not spoken to anyone about the issue or the encounter with the woman at the park. Yet within the week, new donations to the building fund began coming in.

One afternoon a member of our church stopped by the offices and proceeded to tell me God had spoken to him about doing something special for the church. He took a check from his pocket and placed it in my hands. It was for $100,000. God had told him to give that amount, and he was obedient to His prompting. I was blown away by his generosity, but more than that, I was blown away by how God orchestrated every bit of it to meet our immediate needs.

We settled with each of the subcontractors. They simply asked that we pay their expenses because they knew we had been done wrong just as they had been. In the end, the church paid the contractor once, which should have paid the subcontractors, and then we paid the subcontractors directly. It may not have been our responsibility to pay them, but we wanted to do the right thing. The reputation of Rock Springs Church was more important than anything else. And because we did the right thing, several of those subcontractors began coming to our church on Sunday mornings. What seemed like our worst nightmare at the time was life-changing for several men and their families.

God exceeded every expectation and did more than we could have ever imagined through construction of the new sanctuary. He didn't just get us through the difficult circumstances; He defied the odds by using every seemingly negative obstacle for our good and His glory. Within the first two years in the new sanctuary, the average attendance almost doubled from 939 to 1,542.

God didn't stop with amazing growth in attendance; He also defied all odds in the finances of the church. The $4,000,000 loan that was supposed to take 30 years to pay off was fully paid in three years and nine months—all with "the wrong clientele of people." And the building I couldn't imagine filling is now filled for three Sunday morning services each week with overflow seating in the lobby. God was showing me exactly what the Bible means when it says He can "do far more abundantly than all that we ask or think" (Ephesians 3:20).

I'm so glad I never allowed the opinions of others to get in the way of God's vision. When I sought advice from church growth specialists in the 1990s, they told me Rock Springs Church would be "lucky" to ever reach an average attendance of 300. They also said we would reach that number only by closing our doors and merging with other churches in the community.

Then while at a Braves game with a well-known leadership expert— if I said his name, you would recognize it immediately—I eagerly sought advice concerning what I could do to get Rock Springs Church to the next level. His advice? "I recommend you leave your church." He didn't see how a church our size in such a rural area could ever get to the next level.

Come to find out, I didn't need the right clientele of people—I had God's people. I didn't need luck to see growth in attendance—I had the Lord's hand. I didn't need to leave my church—I let God lead His church.

All glory be to God for how He provided for Rock Springs Church and defied all odds. All gratitude is owed to its members, who have given me the extreme privilege of being their pastor. I have always said, "I don't believe great preachers build great churches; I believe great churches build great preachers." As God called me to cast each vision, the people were faithful in providing support every step of the way.

God's Work Draws Attention

Word began to spread about what God was doing at Rock Springs Church, and in 2006, the Associated Press expressed interest in writing an article about us. The article detailed how our average weekly attendance was five times greater than the population of our area. Many found it amazing that the church attracted members from every surrounding county, with some people driving over an hour to attend

Sunday service. The only explanation we could give was the same statement Dr. Jerry Falwell Sr. made the first time he drove onto our campus: "This is a miracle ministry!"

Tommy Barnett, pastor and cofounder of the famed Dream Center in Los Angeles, was asked what he would do differently if he could do things over again. He said, "I would dream bigger dreams."[1] With a successful megachurch, bestselling books, and life-changing Dream Centers, it's hard to imagine how Tommy Barnett could possibly dream bigger. But his response has served as motivation for me to keep expecting the incredible from God. I never want to stop dreaming and casting vision for all that God can do at Rock Springs Church.

God proved all of the experts wrong and defied all odds in the growth of our church. Many people may have thought our little rural church had finally reached its peak, but with God, the peak is beyond our range of sight. The construction of the Butler Building and the new sanctuary was just the start to all God would do at Rock Springs Church in the years to come. He had only just begun, and He would soon baffle everyone with His idea of growth.

Let's be honest—no one likes change. Well, I take that back. Wet babies like change. That's about the only time when people look forward to change without apprehension and discomfort.

Former US Congressman Bruce Barton once said, "When you're through changing, you're through."[2] His words are true for our everyday lives as well as in our walk with Christ—change is a requirement for moving forward. It seems as though most people are on board with the exciting new changes in society, such as technology, business, and fashion, but individual change is a topic frequently avoided. Everyone talks about changing the world, but people rarely think about changing themselves. The refusal to change, however, always limits the potential for progress.

Second Corinthians 3:18 says. "We all, with unveiled face, beholding the glory of the Lord, are being transformed into the same image from one degree of glory to another. For this comes from the Lord who is the Spirit." God is all about change. He wants to continually change us from glory to glory as He transforms us into the image of His Son. While changing from glory to glory sounds like a wonderful experience, it most likely will be uncomfortable at times. And most people like to avoid anything that takes them out of their comfort zone.

I have experienced so much change throughout my life, and I've come to realize that the only thing that stays the same is the fact that everything changes.

When I was a young boy, that older couple I sometimes stayed with kept a bowl of water on the kitchen table with a dipper inside it. When I said I was thirsty, they told me, "Run on into the kitchen and dip you out a drink." Then I used the dipper to draw up some water and drink directly from it before putting it back into the bowl. Oh, how things have changed! Now I grab a glass from the cabinet and fill it with water from the refrigerator door. The need for me to drink water is timeless, but the method for my drinking it changed. I haven't stopped drinking water just because I no longer use a bowl and a dipper to get a drink. Only the method I use to drink it has changed drastically over time.

Here's what I know: If we're not careful, we'll miss out on the very things we need because the required method isn't what we're used to or prefer. God will take us from glory to glory—from greatness to greatness—when we willingly accept change. And He will defy the odds in your life when you understand these three truths: there is no growth without change, no change without opposition and loss, and no loss without pain.

No Growth Without Change

An experiment conducted by plant scientists found that doubling a plant's pot size results in an average 43 percent growth increase.[3] So significant growth occurs for the plant when its environment has changed. I believe the same is true for humans—significant growth occurs when we're open to change in our physical and spiritual circumstances. This was certainly true for the growth at Rock Springs Church.

I believe the greatest threat to future success is current success.

When we grew to two services in the old chapel and a new building for Sunday school, the congregation was blown away by the success we'd achieved. Reaching more than 300 people in attendance on Sunday mornings was beyond all we could have ever imagined for our little country church. But when the time came to make even bigger changes to accommodate future growth, the people struggled to move forward.

Babe Ruth once said, "Yesterday's home runs don't win today's game"[4]—a great statement to quote but a principle difficult to live out. When good things happen to us, it can be easy to hold on for dear life out of fear that new successes won't come. No doubt we've all experienced times when we've stepped out in faith and seen wonderful growth and success. Yet we become fearful that our next big step won't result in the same outcome. We cling to the most recent growth and refuse to look ahead for new opportunities to experience even greater success.

Maybe you struggled in your career for years before receiving a promotion, but trusting God to take you even further seems like a long shot. Or perhaps you finally have a close friend after spending many lonely years praying for godly friends, but you still find it hard to get involved in ministry or open up to others in small groups. Success that comes after hardship can become a crutch in the future. While it's okay to celebrate and praise God for the good things He's done, you must continue believing that He has even more for you in store.

As I mentioned earlier in this book, God promises in Isaiah 43:19, "Behold, I am doing a new thing; now it springs forth, do you not perceive it? I will make a way in the wilderness and rivers in the desert." Notice that God doesn't say "I did a new thing" or "I will do a new thing." He says "I am doing a new thing" because His actions of renewal are constant. The same promise made thousands of years ago remains true for you and me today. God is doing a new thing for us every day, but we become so focused on our last success or remain so fearful of uncomfortable changes that we miss out on the new things He wants to do in and through our lives.

In order for God to defy the odds, you must be willing to accept any changes He wants to make. He is doing a new thing, which will spring forth with growth you never could have imagined or planned for yourself. Let God replant you in uncomfortable territory, because He will multiply all that you entrust to Him.

No Change Without Opposition and Loss

One time a pastor said to me, "I have great news! I changed something in my church, and nobody got upset." I didn't want to ruin his excitement, but if he changed something and nobody got upset, he didn't really change anything. With change comes opposition, especially when that change affects multiple people. Everyone has opinions and preferences, and people will share their commentary about whatever it is you decide to change.

I can't help but think back to services in the old chapel when we sang from hymnals. But new families had joined the church, and the crowd was more diverse in age than ever. As I sang along to "When We All Get to Heaven," I looked out across the sanctuary and saw my precious, teenage daughter standing beside Barbara, staring straight ahead.

I dropped my head and said to God, *I'm losing her, Lord.* And He said, *Yes, and you're losing many others, too, because you refuse to change.*

Making a change to the worship music on Sunday mornings is always met with strong opposition. People get used to the way the service runs and don't want anyone messing with their routine, and I knew adding contemporary worship songs would result in a lot of opposition and even some loss. Over the years, people have left our church for a variety of reasons, and the majority of the time it had something to do with changes they didn't like or want. Losing members is never something I enjoy or take lightly, but pleasing God will always take priority over pleasing people.

The same will be true in your life. God's plans may not always make sense to those around you. He may lead you in a completely different career path or require great changes for your family at the most inconvenient time. Saying yes to His calling may be incredibly difficult because of the responses you know you will get from others. But here are the facts: You will have critics, and you will experience loss when following God. Yet you will never experience a greater sense of peace than when you are right in the center of God's will.

You must remember that everything nice has a price, and the price for following God in a fallen world can seem so high when it results in opposition that leads to loss. People and opportunities certainly come into your life for a reason, but many times they stay for only a season. Refusing to change because you're worried about what others will think or that others might leave you will only limit God in what He can do in your life. While growth requires change, the change will be followed by opposition, and then probably loss. And whether great or small, that loss causes pain.

No Loss Without Pain

I have never been a *Name it, claim it; believe it, receive it; blab it, grab it* preacher because the Bible is clear that we will experience pain and difficulty in this life. God never promised us preservation; He promised evacuation. Becoming a Christian does not mean we are exempt from life's storms. I'm convinced that for Christians, it's exactly the opposite—we encounter more hardships. Maintaining our Christian walk requires us to be different from the rest of the world. Jesus comes into our hearts and changes us for the better, but not everyone will see it that way. They may support your salvation but not your changed lifestyle.

College football fans in my state are pretty serious when it comes to cheering on their beloved Georgia Bulldogs, but everyone who knows me understands that I am a Tennessee fan through and through. I promise you I've never made a joke about those Bulldogs without receiving a whole lot of jeers and judgment. Being the odd-fan-out on game day ensures that I get an awful lot of flak from every Georgia fan.

Christians are a lot like the odd-fan-out; we're cheering for the opposing team in this world, which means we'll be met with quite a bit of judgment and pain. A lot more than a championship trophy is at stake, though, so the pain associated with a loss is much greater. With new levels come new devils. Just as a sports team faces stronger competition the closer it gets to the championship, Christians experience more difficult trials the longer we walk with and the closer we get to Jesus.

You will quit growing only when you refuse to push through the pain. Change isn't always immediate, but criticism is. You must be willing to put in the hard work and push through the pain that comes with following Christ. Jeremiah 12:5 says, "If you have raced with men on foot, and they have wearied you, how will you compete with horses? And if in a safe land you are so trusting, what will you do in the thicket of the Jordan?" Your foundation must be Jesus and your strength must be found in God's Word if you are to endure the pain that comes as you grow in your walk with Christ.

To see God defy the odds, you must embrace change, and significant growth will occur when you accept the loss and endure the pain that comes with change. God has so much more for you! It doesn't matter how much He's already done—He is doing more. Your last success is just one of many more to come. Stepping out in faith and allowing God to change you and your circumstances will only result in exponential growth.

PRAY FOR THE DESIRES OF YOUR HEART

G rowing up where I did in Tennessee, I never really imagined life outside of those mountains. It seemed pretty clear that my life would never look much different from those around me, so I never expected big things to happen. I reserved any ideas for nighttime dreams. As a kid, I prayed for God to move only when I found myself in terrible situations, like when my mother was in danger of a beating from Bill or he was about to beat me. Otherwise, I prayed to comfort myself, not to actually talk to God or rely on His ability to work on my behalf. Although as you'll see later in this chapter, I did ask him for a particular husband for my mother.

Even after coming to know the Lord and beginning to preach, I didn't expect God to do big things with my life. I just figured He would use me to pastor a little church and reach as many people as I could for Jesus right there in those mountains. Then God's calling me to Georgia was bigger than anything I had ever imagined. Before moving there, I had never seen an ocean beach or eaten at a Mexican restaurant. Barbara and I were just hill people, and life outside of those hills had never really crossed my mind. But all along God had even bigger plans to take me farther than a few hundred miles south.

Hoping for the Holy Land

Seeing God move in mighty ways during my early years at Rock Springs Church lifted my faith and led me to begin praying for bigger and bigger things. Certainly I spent much of my time asking God to grow me as a person and for people to know Jesus, but I also began praying about an opportunity I had always longed for. I asked God to allow me to visit the Holy Land. I desperately wanted to walk where Jesus had walked and see the Bible come to life right before my eyes. It seemed like such a lofty goal, because Barbara and I didn't have the money for a trip to Israel. But I just prayed for the opportunity and left the details up to God.

Lo and behold, God worked it out. Members of Rock Springs Church came together to raise the funds to send me to Israel, and I was able to travel with a group of people that included a pastor friend of mine from Tennessee. Many wonderful things that changed my life happened during that trip, and God used a particular event to put so many of His other plans in motion.

One evening our guide took us to see the Jordan River, but he said it was too late in the day for anyone to be baptized. I told him, "Look, I'm just a country preacher, and I'll never get to come back. This is a once-in-a-lifetime trip for me. So my friend and I are going down into the water to baptize each other." And that's just what we did. With very little daylight left, my pastor friend and I waded into the water of the Jordan River and baptized each other. Once we were finished, we turned around to find a long line of people waiting to experience baptism too. We baptized every person that evening despite how dark it had become.

One night toward the end of our trip, I was walking through our hotel when I ran into Dr. Jerry Falwell Sr. It was such an honor to meet him, and I thought, *It would be wonderful to have him come preach at Rock Springs Church someday.* I never suspected a chance encounter with him in a hotel in Israel was a tiny connection God was making for my future.

Ten years after that trip, I wrote to Dr. Falwell and invited him to come speak at our church, then communicated back and forth with his executive assistant for several months before confirming a 2006 date. After leaving the big city and driving for many miles, passing thousands of acres of farmland and pine trees, most people are amazed at what they see when they pull into the parking lot of the church. No one expects a church our size to be thriving in the middle of nowhere. And upon Dr. Falwell's arrival on our campus, he said, "Benny, I know why you're doing so well out here...the devil hasn't found you yet!"

You see, there's a difference between praying for things to happen and working to make them happen yourself. It can be tempting to pray about our desires once and then get to work on figuring out how to accomplish them on our own. For instance, people can become consumed with connecting with the right people. But if we focus on connecting with God, He will connect us with the right people. That's exactly what happened on that trip to Israel—God began piecing together connections for my future that would eventually lead me back to Israel many times.

I never imagined that I would take ten more trips after that first one. I never thought God would allow me to preach at the Garden Tomb and baptize hundreds of people in the Jordan River. What if I had never prayed those prayers? What if I had not asked God to grant me my desire to visit the Holy Land? Just because I didn't think a trip like that would ever be possible for me didn't mean God thought so.

Instead of allowing my insecurities and limited sight to get in the way, I decided to continue praying for the desires of my heart regardless of how impossible they seemed. If our hopes, dreams, and desires are not impossible for us, they are an insult to God. We should be praying for what can be accomplished only with His help.

Meeting a Legendary Man

Another great desire of my heart was to one day meet Billy Graham. I couldn't tell you how many times I prayed for the opportunity. One day a staff member at Rock Springs Church who traveled with me quite a bit came to my office and said, "Several times I've overheard you praying about God making it work out in North Carolina. Are you planning to leave Rock Springs to pastor a different church up there?" I explained that I'd been praying about going to North Carolina to meet Billy Graham for a very long time.

A dear friend of mine, Dr. James Merritt, was one of the few people who knew about those prayers. James was scheduled to speak at the Billy Graham Training Center at The Cove in Asheville, North Carolina, and he requested a meeting for us with Dr. Graham. I can remember my exact location when James called to say our meeting had been confirmed for a specific date as long as Dr. Graham's health permitted—the George H.W. Bush Presidential Library in Houston, Texas. I'm sure you can guess what my prayer was leading up to that meeting: *Lord, be with Dr. Graham's health!*

It seemed as if every obstacle that could come between us and our meeting did in fact arise. Not only were we at the mercy of Dr. Graham's fluctuating health condition, but the day before we were to leave for North Carolina, Barbara's daddy died. I was so upset over the loss of my father-in-law that I told Barbara I wasn't going to North Carolina. I wanted to stay with her during such a difficult time. But Barbara was adamant that I go. She said, "Benny, I have been praying about this opportunity for years, just as you have. You are going to North Carolina tomorrow. You'll have time to meet with Dr. Graham and be back for the funeral. You're going!"

Our prayers were answered yes. James and I met with Billy Graham in his modest home the very next day, and after introductions and handshakes, I sat down in front of Dr. Graham and began to cry. I was humbled and honored to be in the presence of one of the greatest preachers to have ever lived.

I believe it's wise to learn from experience but even wiser to learn from the experience of others. And it's not nearly as painful. Who better to learn from than Billy Graham? Before leaving that meeting, I asked him one final question: "I'm a pastor, and I serve as president of our denomination. I oversee a lot of preachers and try to encourage them as much as I can. What advice would you give me?"

Dr. Graham said, "You go back and tell those preachers to preach the cross, just preach the cross." That advice has been such an encouragement to me and many other pastors over the years.

Seeing God grant the desires of my heart has led me to encourage others to never give up on what they're praying for. Continually pray for the desires of your heart. Be persistent in your prayer life regardless of how long it takes to receive an answer. In Luke 18:1, Jesus taught His disciples to "always pray and never give up" (NLT). God wants us to be like the persistent widow who wore out the judge with her persistent requests or the blind beggar who continued yelling for Jesus to have mercy on him. Both the widow and the blind beggar never gave up on their desires even though everyone tried to discourage them.

My Childhood Hero

While many of my greatest desires have been ministry-based in some way, others I prayed for may seem silly to people. But whether the desires of your heart relate to your Christian walk or are simply things you've always dreamed of, "let your requests be made known to God" (Philippians 4:6). He cares about your every desire and wants you to trust Him with each one—even a childhood dream that may seem silly to ask for as an adult.

Out of all the sports I watched and played when I was young, I loved football the most. The Dallas Cowboys was my favorite team, and Roger Staubach was my favorite player. I vividly remember lying in bed late at night asking God to let my mother marry Roger. I just knew we could live as one happy family if she did. When Bill got to drinking and taking his anger out on Mama, with all seriousness I would ask God to make this marriage to my football hero work out. As a small child, I thought that marriage would be the answer to all of our problems.

Of course, as an adult, I realized the ridiculousness of that nighttime prayer because we had no way of ever meeting such a celebrity—not to mention that he was already happily married! But I also realized how easy it was for me to pray for the purest desires of my heart.

In 2013, I had the opportunity to preach in Dallas. As I prepared for the trip, I thought back to that innocent prayer about Mama marrying Roger Staubach. While of course I no longer hoped for anything like that to happen, I still had a great desire to meet my hero. I knew it was a long shot, but I wrote him a letter telling him about the prayer I prayed so many nights as a kid. Then I just prayed that God would allow a meeting with him to happen while I was in Texas.

A few days before I left for Dallas, I received a phone call from Roger's assistant letting me know Roger wanted to meet me while I was in town. I couldn't believe what I was hearing. A dream I'd had for so many years was going to come true. We agreed on a time, and the meeting was set. I was going to meet my childhood hero.

Savannah Abigail was going with me on this trip, making it even more special. We had a tradition of visiting baseball stadiums together, and we were planning to see the Texas Rangers play. I was scheduled to preach one night and then go to the baseball game the next night. But we would be meeting Roger Staubach in between those two events.

Oftentimes, people get a chance to meet their childhood hero but then wish they never had because the person they admired from afar turned out to be much different. That was definitely not the case when I met Roger Staubach. He was a wonderful man. I knew right away that he was a modest, humble person. As we shook hands, I said, "I'm sure you get many requests for meetings."

His assistant quickly spoke up. "Thousands. He won't tell you that, but he receives thousands of requests."

I said to him, "Mr. Staubach, why did you decide to see me?"

He replied, "I believed your story."

Savannah Abigail and I were able to talk with him for more than two hours, and it was such a wonderful experience that I will never forget it. As we were wrapping up, Roger asked me, "Do you come to Dallas a lot?"

I quickly answered, "Well, I can!"

He proceeded to tell me he had a box at the Dallas Cowboys Stadium and would like to send me a schedule so I could choose a game to attend with him. Yes. Roger Staubach invited me to watch a Dallas Cowboys game with him in his personal box! Later that year, I went back to Dallas to do it. It was a dream come true—a dream that seemed too far-fetched to pray for in the first place. But I have learned to trust God with *all* of the desires of my heart.

◆

Looking back on all of the wonderful things God has done throughout my life, I believe all the more that He chooses to work through the most unlikely people and situations. First Corinthians 1:27 says, "God chose what is foolish in the world to shame the wise; God chose what is weak in the world to shame the strong," and that explains the story of my life so well. There's nothing special about me or my life to cause God to do such amazing works. He's used my life in a mighty way only because I have placed all of my confidence in Him alone.

Reading *Fresh Wind, Fresh Fire* by Jim Cymbala as a young pastor had a greater impact on my prayer life than any other book outside of the Bible. It inspired me to establish Saturday prayer in our sanctuary before Sunday services. I would buy extra copies to hand out to people whenever I could. Our congregation raised money to send me to visit Brooklyn Tabernacle to meet Jim Cymbala. I never could have imagined that years later he would come to preach at Rock Springs Church. And as if that wasn't the most unlikely thing to happen, God later arranged for me to preach at the Brooklyn Tabernacle. Prayer changes everything!

To see God defy all odds in your prayer life, you must have the attitude and belief that He can do anything. There isn't one single thing He can't accomplish, and no details are so complicated that He can't execute His plan with perfection. Pray with conviction for Him to use you in great ways, and that's just what He will do.

Again, in James 4:2 the Bible is clear that "you do not have, because you do not ask." Don't withhold anything from God. Give it all to Him and leave the details, answers, and provisions to Him. I'm convinced you will see God grant the desires of your heart when you ask with abundance, ask with confidence, and ask with praise and gratitude.

Ask with Abundance

Many people have trouble asking God for what they need, so instead, they struggle to complete tasks or endure circumstances on their own. The same can be true when it comes to their hopes and dreams. They settle for what they have because they don't ask God for anything bigger or better.

We all think about our hopes and dreams from time to time, but we rarely pray about them, especially continually. Our greatest desires have a way of taking a backseat to the pressing matters of today, and we simply don't pray for the desires of our hearts as God would want us to. Instead, we dismiss them as unimportant or impossible or shove them to the backs of our minds. But all the while, God wants to leave us speechless with what only He can do.

I'm reminded of a story about a little boy who wanted a brother or sister, so he began praying for that for about three month and then quit. After another six months passed, his father took him to a little window in the hospital. As the curtain was pulled back more and more, he saw three little babies on the other side of the glass—triplets! His father leaned down and said, "Aren't you glad you prayed?" And the little boy responded, "Aren't you glad I stopped after three months?"

In Matthew 7:7, Jesus paints a clear picture of God's heart for giving to His children: "Ask, and it will be given to you; seek, and you will find; knock, and it will be opened to you." And in verse 11—as I mentioned earlier—we're told Jesus also said to the people, "If you then, who are evil, know how to give good gifts to your children, how much more will your Father who is in heaven give good things to those who ask him!" God wants to give you the desires of your heart. He wants to bless you greatly and give abundantly to you. But Matthew 7:7 is very clear in stating the requirement for God's provision—you must ask, seek, and knock.

If God isn't giving to you abundantly, I'm convinced that the only reason is because you aren't asking abundantly. Don't limit His ability to give to you by asking for only your immediate needs or for things you believe He will most likely give you. Ask Him for everything! It's not your job to decide what God does or does not care about. You are His child, and He cares about every tiny detail of your life. He is a good Father, and He wants to give abundantly to His children.

After graduating college, Savannah Abigail moved to Missouri to work with children with special needs. One time when Barbara and I visited her out there, she mentioned that she had been wanting a grill because a lot of her friends were grilling out and she wanted to invite people over. I insisted that we go right then to get her a grill. After all, Walmart was only a mile from her house. We looked at every kind of grill available and found the perfect one, already assembled.

I was thrilled to get my girl a grill, but there was one small problem: It wouldn't fit in our rental car! We tried to maneuver that thing every which way, but it was not going in. I was determined to get that grill back to her house, though, so I went to pushing. I pushed that grill along the side of the highway one whole mile from Walmart back to her house. It was a sight to be seen, and we still laugh about it to this day.

Because she's mine, there's nothing I wouldn't do for Savannah. As I told you before, when I became her father, I knew I would do anything to ensure she had everything she wanted in life. I wanted to give her good gifts as often as possible to the best of my ability, to do everything in my power to support her and make her happy. If a sinner like me wants to give abundantly to my child, how much more does our perfect Father in heaven want to give us abundantly more than we could ever ask for? But we must first ask and ask abundantly.

Ask with Confidence

Developing the habit of praying for the desires of your heart may be an uncomfortable process, but it will be the easiest part. The difficulty comes in truly believing God for everything you ask Him for. Just because you make your requests known to God doesn't mean you fully believe He will grant you the desires of your heart. You can go through the motions without any real expectation.

First John 5:14-15 says, "This is the confidence that we have toward him, that if we ask anything according to his will, he hears us. And if we know that he hears us in whatever we ask, we know that we have the requests that we have asked of him." You can have confidence when praying for the desires of your heart because of who your Father is, not what you deserve to receive. Never base your confidence on whether you have been good enough or have done enough for God to reward you with your desires. Your confidence must come from knowing the truth found in His Word concerning His never-ending love for you.

Because of the insecurities I've always battled, I naturally want to disqualify myself from so many things I would love to see God do in and through my life. If I'm not careful, I can begin thinking He would never do whatever it is for me because of any one of the mistakes I have made over the years. But I continually remind myself that although I did nothing to deserve or earn my salvation, while I was still a sinner God sent His Son to die on a cross so I can spend eternity with Him. Why would I ever think He would give or withhold any good thing from me based on my goodness or ability? It's never about me; it's always about Him!

Not everyone has a crime-to-Christ testimony or some dramatic Damascus Road experience. Maybe you accepted Jesus early in life, grew up in church, and have had a strong relationship with the Lord for many years, yet you still find it difficult to pray for the desires of your heart and truly expect God to grant you those desires. Reflecting on all that God has done in your life and seeing how He has protected and blessed you in so many ways may make it difficult for you to ask for anything bigger or better than what you have. You may think you've already been the recipient of so many blessings that it's hard for you to truly believe God will do even more.

Wherever you find yourself on the "bad past" scale, you must realize that when God looks at you, He sees only the blood of Jesus. God is immeasurable, and so are His gifts and blessings. He has no set number of blessings for each person, and His love is never based on your performance. Keep seeking Him and pouring out your heart in faith because He can grant every desire of your heart and more.

When you confidently believe that God not only wants to give you good gifts but that He delights in giving you the greatest desires of your heart, you will experience Him in unbelievable ways, and things you never thought possible will happen. And you will experience greater faith and a deeper relationship with your heavenly Father. Confidently believe Him for more, because He is the God of abundantly more.

Ask with Praise and Gratitude

A.W. Tozer once said, "If God takes away everything I have, I will love Him anyway. I will praise Him even if He slays me. We have to overcome, because the overcomer will be able to stand on that terrible day."[1] Our posture toward God should be one of continual praise regardless of our circumstances or disappointments. Whether or not our prayers are answered as we prefer, our praise should never cease and our confidence should never waver because God is good. And that will never change.

There is *always* reason enough to praise God, and when you ask Him for the desires of your heart, praise should begin long before an answer is ever received. Express gratitude for all He's done and for all He will do even though you have yet to see it. And if it doesn't happen as you hoped, praise Him for knowing better than you what is best for your life. Gratitude produces blessing, and God will reward your attitude of praise even when circumstances don't turn out as planned or when desires of your heart have not been granted as you thought they would.

The author of Psalm 77:3 says, "I remembered God, and was troubled; I complained, and my spirit was overwhelmed" (NKJV). When we groan and grumble, we become overwhelmed by all going on around us. I'm convinced that the more we complain, the less we obtain. You see, there's a difference between thanksgiving and praise. Thanksgiving is expressing gratitude for what God has done in your life, but praise is expressing esteem simply for who He is. We will experience a greater peace and a deeper confidence in God when we choose to praise Him ahead of our requests.

I'm reminded of how Jesus healed the ten lepers in Luke 17. Although all ten of the men received healing, only one returned to Jesus, who said in verse 18, "Was no one found to return and give praise to God except this foreigner?" Verse 19 explains what praise does for us: "[Jesus] said to him, 'Rise and go your way; your faith has made you well.'" This second verse suggests there's a difference in being healed and being made well. I don't know about you, but I don't want to settle for healing when I can experience complete wellness. I want to be made whole!

God wants to grant the desires of your heart, but more than that He wants closeness with you. His number one concern for your life will always be holiness over happiness. Yes, you can have both, but holiness will always take priority. Praise positions our hearts to seek God's will above our own, and only then will we be able to develop a relationship with Him that transcends circumstantial faith. As your heart aligns with His, your greatest desires will mirror His plans for your life.

The Enemy wants you to believe you are unworthy of your greatest desires, so he wants you to focus on all of the reasons you don't deserve God's blessings. But we already know he's a liar. Thoughts of that kind are not from God; that's not His voice you're hearing. You are God's precious child, and He wants to give good gifts to His children. Don't disqualify yourself because of the lies you've been led to believe about yourself. Dig into the truth of God's Word and take hold of the promises He's made for His children.

You will see God defy the odds in your life when you commit to pushing past any doubt or discomfort and begin asking abundantly for the desires of your heart. Believe with confidence that He has more than enough in store for you and that there is no limit to what He can and will do if you will let Him move and work. Maintain an attitude of gratitude simply because of who He is and what He has already done for you. So much greatness is ahead for you—ask, believe, and praise Him for it all.

THE BEST IS YET TO COME

n John 14:12, Jesus said to the apostles, "I tell you the truth, anyone who believes in me will do the same works I have done, and even greater works, because I am going to be with the Father" (NLT). So "anyone who believes" will do greater works. In case you don't fully understand, anyone means *anyone!* Every single believer. No Christian is specifically favored with the distinct privilege of doing greater works than Jesus; this promise is for every individual who believes in the Lord.

God had even greater works in mind through growing and blessing Rock Springs Church as well. Church attendance and ministry involvement continued to grow to the point of our needing even more room, and we have been in a building project ever since!

Construction on the Branch—a 4.2 million-dollar building—began in 2007 and allowed additional space for small groups and student ministry. Today, the Branch is the most heavily used building on our campus. We have small groups meeting on Sunday and throughout the week, a youth service with more than a hundred kids meeting weekly, and Rock Springs Christian Academy middle school students are housed there daily. It also serves as one of our satellite campuses on Sunday mornings.

With a significant number of people driving more than 30 miles to attend church services and small group activities, God led me to step out in faith to establish additional campuses throughout middle Georgia. And to think, we were once concerned about being able to get people in our area to attend!

God continues to grow Rock Springs Church and its ministries in ways no one could have ever imagined. With the addition of multiple campuses, a 14,500-square-foot gymnasium, a three-story children's facility, and a state-of-the-art recreational complex, family life and community involvement at Rock Springs Church has multiplied and spread from throughout our original campus to many surrounding counties.

Each and every building and ministry at Rock Springs Church is from God. When discussing the amazing miracles that have taken place over the years, I've often said, "To God be the glory, to the Rock Springs Church people be the credit, and the privilege has been mine!" No special giftedness on my part has come into play, only God's good hand and perfect provision. If He can use someone like me, He can use anyone. Every good thing that has happened in our church has had nothing to do with what I have done but everything to do with who God is.

You've probably heard the saying "The bigger they are, the harder they fall," which can be true in many contexts. In Christian leadership, there is no guarantee of permanence—any platform or pulpit can disappear in a moment. The same can be true of any position of leadership; circumstances can change in the blink of an eye. Jesus is our only guarantee, in good times and bad. When hard times come and heavy hits are taken, the Lord must be our only refuge.

I encourage every reader to give your entire life to God, your dreams, goals, fears, family, insecurities, strongholds—every single thing—and He will do the unexplainable. As others have said, God doesn't call the equipped; He equips the called. He offers salvation to everyone from the uttermost to the gutter-most. While you may see only your past, God sees your potential. And then just when you think He's accomplished all that can be done with your life, He will do even more!

Facing the Greatest Odds

While it may seem impossible to do greater works than Jesus did, we must understand that we live in a time of greater population, greater technology, and greater Holy Spirit power. Joel 2:28 details the Lord's promise for the last days: "I will pour out my Spirit upon all people" (NLT). I believe we're living in the last days and that God has given us greater opportunity to reach the lost and impact His kingdom, so it's more important than ever before to believe Him for great things and expect Him to move in mighty ways!

When many people probably thought He had accomplished all that could be done at Rock Springs Church through building programs, ministry opportunities, and community outreach, God decided to do the unexplainable once again.

In March of 2020, the arrival of COVID-19 in the United States certainly caused our church to anticipate hard times and heavy hits. With an average attendance of more than 6,000 people no longer attending services at any of our locations, it was assumed that the average amount received in weekly tithes and offerings would decrease significantly. The odds of us making it through the shutdown without financial cuts seemed impossible. My immediate concern was that our pastors and staff may receive pay cuts—or worse, layoffs. Decisions that impact the livelihood of others are the most stressful and difficult to make. The only way I could handle such circumstances was to get on my knees in prayer.

When Rock Springs Church closed its doors for in-person services, I knew everyone would look to me for clarity and guidance concerning how the church would move forward in such unprecedented circumstances. I walked through the doors of our church offices early in the morning on the first Sunday after the shutdown, and as I turned the corner down the main hallway early that morning, I saw many of our pastors standing along the walls. I could see the fear and concern written all over their faces. They were scared of the unknown. Honestly, I was scared too. It felt as if the weight of the world sat squarely on my shoulders. I wanted to give them definite answers that would ease their fears, but I had no way of knowing what the future held for our church. So I did the only thing I knew to do—I sought God.

It's the responsibility of the leader to cast the vision, and God led me to encourage our staff with the phrase "faith over fear." They all committed to praying together daily and seeking God moment by moment, continuing to trust that He was who He had always been—Jehovah Tsaba, our warrior. We were facing a battle down here, but we knew the battle would be won up there.

I believe God-vision will always produce provision, and our greatest priority at Rock Springs Church is keeping our eyes on Jesus. Even when unimaginable circumstances threaten to destroy us, our focus must remain on our Father, and we must maintain faith over fear. Second Timothy 1:7 reminds us, "God gave us a spirit not of fear but of power and love and self-control." Therefore, we must rely on the power of the Holy Spirit to sustain us in difficult times, seek to love others in the midst of division, and exhibit self-control regardless of how others respond to difficult situations.

Instead of making immediate changes and hurried preparations for the negative effects that could come with the shutdown, I decided to trust more and give more both in ministry and in my personal life. As a church, we sought additional opportunities to help communities and churches in the weeks and months ahead. We have always been a church that supports others by generously giving to small churches and community programs, and we were not going to let fear of the unknown keep us from continuing to serve the Lord. And Barbara and I decided to increase our weekly tithes.

While the church was closed for face-to-face services for nine weeks, the staff at Rock Springs Church continued to work six days a week connecting with members regularly, served community healthcare workers, and provided quality services via our live stream capabilities. We operated under the "whatever" principle of Colossians 3:23: "Whatever you do, work heartily, as for the Lord and not for men." Every single staff member took on new responsibilities and maintained a "whatever it takes" mindset. I preached three separate services each Sunday morning as always and made visits.

We worked harder than ever, doing all we could and trusting God to do all we couldn't. As we continued to be the hands and feet of Jesus, He defied the odds for our church once again.

Although the people of Rock Springs Church weren't physically meeting in our buildings, they were faithful to gather online every Sunday and Wednesday to worship the Lord. God blessed us with the ability to live stream services through various outlets, which resulted in almost one million views over the nine-week period. Not only were people faithful to gather, but they were faithful to give. Giving of tithes and offerings during the nine-week shutdown was higher than ever before. God completely blew us away with His provision!

As a result of increased giving, we were able to support several smaller churches who had no live streaming capabilities and were experiencing financial difficulty due to the lack of face-to-face attendance. Our church also donated meals to more than 20 local medical facilities to support healthcare workers on the front lines putting in overtime to care for sick people. As we sought opportunities to support others, God continued to provide the necessary resources. He was Jehovah Jireh, our provider. I believe God doesn't want to simply get things to us but to get them through us. He wants us to freely give to others what He has given to us.

I believed God for provision—He had never failed to provide at any point in my life or ministry. Despite my initial concern, I was not at all surprised when giving was up. And I wasn't surprised that our members were tuning in for services each week. Yet God moved in two distinct ways that did take me by surprise—completely. Not only did He show up but He showed out!

Pastors manned the phones and social media communications to connect and pray with people as I preached services each Sunday. I always gave an invitation for salvation at the end of each service, which allowed people watching to repeat the sinner's prayer and accept Jesus as their Lord and Savior. Whether they called the church or let us know on an online platform, people watching each service every single week told us they'd accepted Jesus. Over the nine-week period, 343 people came to know Christ!

God also moved in a mighty way by reaching people from all over the world through our live streaming services. Each week our pre-service announcers asked viewers to let us know their locations. We simply wanted to be praying for them and their communities. We never could have predicted responses from so many countries around the world—48! People from Canada and the United Kingdom also contacted us to express their desire to become a member of Rock Springs Church! Now, because of this growth, we've established an online campus and online small groups where people from all around the world connect. I'm not sure how our overseas viewers understand anything that comes out of my Southern mouth, but I'm so glad to have them as a part of our church.

As if God's incredible provision for our day-to-day work in ministry wasn't enough, He allowed a longtime vision of mine to become a reality in the midst of these circumstances. Billy Graham's advice to "preach the cross" made a huge impact on my life after meeting with him in 2011, and his words inspired the vision for Rock Springs Church to one day have a 120-foot cross on its campus. Our congregation had been so faithful to give in our 2019 Manger Offering at Christmastime, which went toward the cross project, an outdoor baptistry, and a prayer garden right on our campus.

In July of 2020, the cross was erected, and people drove from miles around to sit or kneel to pray. It's been such a blessing to see families gathering in prayer, small groups meeting for Bible study, and special ceremonies such as weddings and memorial services taking place at the foot of the cross. As the outdoor baptistry was completed in the months to come, people were able to experience baptism at the foot of the cross. The hope of the cross is the answer to all of the adversity and hardships people face in this life. I have always said that I want Rock Springs Church to be the hardest place for people to go to hell from, and the cross on our campus is just one more way for us to impact our community and point others to Jesus.

Jesus's message in John 14:12—that anyone who believes will do greater works than He did while He was here on earth—is evident when looking at what God did through the people and pastors of Rock

Springs Church during our most difficult time. Greater technology led to reaching a greater population, and a greater Holy Spirit power changed lives in the most unbelievable ways. I am incredibly grateful to have witnessed all Christ has done in my life and in the life of Rock Springs Church.

Difficult seasons teach important and powerful lessons. Shutting our doors for services was the hardest decision I have ever had to make. Preaching to an empty room left me feeling disconnected from the people at times. A good shepherd smells like sheep, and a good pastor is close to his people. But even though shutting the doors created distance and difficulty, it also helped me realize how much I had taken for granted. Never again will I take for granted a full sanctuary or shaking hands and hugging necks with the wonderful people of Rock Springs Church. I'll thank God for every Sunday I get to walk through the doors of the church to preach and love on people. I will cherish every moment I spend face-to-face with people worshipping and fellowshipping together.

God wants to defy the odds in every life, but many times people can't get past complaining about their circumstances long enough for Him to show them He's working things together for their good. There's a lesson to be learned in every difficult trial, and transformation is waiting to take place. God used the most difficult moment for our church to bring forth an incredible transformation in how we connect and serve God's people worldwide. I believe we can change the world right from Rock Springs Church.

In the early days of our church, it was impossible to imagine God reaching multiple counties much less reaching multiple countries. Today, without a doubt, I know He can defy any and all odds that stack against a person, an organization, or a situation. I also know that the greatest days for Rock Springs Church are ahead, that the best is yet to come. God has even greater things in store, and we believe Him to guide and provide every step of the way.

◆

The same is true for you—your greatest days are ahead and the best is yet to come. You must believe God for bigger and better, because defying the odds should always be God-sized. When God defies the odds in your personal life, it is always for the purpose of His kingdom. Therefore, you must be aggressively others-minded in order to see the bigger picture.

Philippians 3:14 tells us exactly what our focus should be. Paul writes, "I press on toward the goal for the prize of the upward call of God in Christ Jesus." The goal is to become like Jesus—not in one area of our lives but in all areas. God defies the odds in those who press on toward that goal. So if being like Jesus is the goal, we must place priority on giving, obedience, the authority of God's Word, and love.

Giving

I'm convinced that God won't give something to you if He can't get it through you. Romans 8:28-29 is clear in God's purpose—He works all things together for our good because He wants to conform us to the image of Jesus. And we are never more like Jesus than when we're giving. Jesus set the example for giving when He went to the cross to pay for our sins. God is not concerned with equal giving but with equal sacrifice.

Jesus explained the sacrifice of giving in Mark 12:43-44, when He told His disciples, "Truly, I say to you, this poor widow has put in more than all those who are contributing to the offering box. For they all contributed out of their abundance, but she out of her poverty has put in everything she had, all she had to live on." While the amount of her offering didn't come close to what others were giving, her sacrifice was much greater.

If the goal is to become more like Jesus, you must give all you have with the right attitude. Second Corinthians 9:7 is clear about the motivation necessary behind all giving: "Each one must give as he has decided in his heart, not reluctantly or under compulsion, for God loves a cheerful giver." While your gift doesn't have to be financial—you can give of your time, talents, and treasure—it should cost you something, and God expects you to give it freely with a cheerful attitude. You shouldn't be so focused on your priorities that you give God what's left over or complain about what you have to offer. He wants you to gladly give of your firstfruits.

Nor should your giving be circumstantial. Fear or hardship shouldn't determine your decision to give. Yes, if your financial situation changes or your schedule becomes more demanding, you may have to make adjustments to your giving, but you shouldn't cease to give out of fear or difficulty. After all, Jesus's decision to give His all on the cross was not affected by His emotions or circumstances.

Obedience

There is no becoming like Jesus without a commitment to obedience. Philippians 2:8 says of Christ, "Being found in human form, he humbled himself by becoming obedient to the point of death, even death on a cross." Jesus didn't seek new circumstances or deny the purpose God had given Him; He humbled Himself and was obedient right where He was.

Many times we're concerned with seeking a new path or acquiring more information before moving forward in obedience. But God has already given us everything we need to thrive in His calling on our lives. We don't need to learn more or acquire more; we need only to be obedient with the information and skills we already have. The truth is this: We are educated far above our level of obedience.

Regarding the first commandment in Exodus 20:3—"You shall have no other gods before me"—D.L. Moody once said, "If men were true to this commandment, obedience to the remaining nine would follow naturally."[1] Obedience can be achieved only through closeness with God, but when achieved it will take care of every other area of life. In complete obedience we experience God's love, assurance, power, and blessing.

We have no problem being obedient when circumstances are pleasant, yet we struggle when obedience threatens to bring discomfort or even suffering. Fear has a way of penetrating every area of our lives, causing us to become hesitant in obeying the Lord. Refusing to let fear and discomfort determine your obedience is the only way to maintain peace in difficult seasons. Jesus knew the immense suffering He would have to endure if He remained obedient to God, but He also knew that no amount of suffering on earth could compare to the pain of turning away from His Father.

The Authority of God's Word

The key to becoming like Jesus and seeing God work in mighty ways is found in the authority of His Word. While the Bible holds the answers to any and all situations we could ever face, research shows that only 9 percent of adults read it daily.[2] We have access to the solution for all of life's problems, but we often seek the easiest solution that requires the least amount of effort on our part.

Second Timothy 3:16 explains that "all Scripture is breathed out by God and profitable for teaching, for reproof, for correction, and for training in righteousness." Did you notice all the ways the Bible is profitable for us? So although it doesn't seem so to most people, studying God's Word should be our greatest priority. Notice I said studying the Bible, not reading it. That's how we can make sure we benefit from it. Simply reading information may produce knowledge, but studying information ensures we obtain *true* knowledge and deep understanding. It's not so important that you get through the Bible but that the Bible gets through you and into you. Getting into your Bible isn't enough. When God's Word becomes more than a quick-skim answer key or book of good quotes, transformation can take place in your life.

Hearing Scripture references at church on Sunday morning won't be enough to get you through the week. Again, James 1:22 says, "Be doers of the word, and not hearers only, deceiving yourselves." While this may seem obvious, you can't do what you don't know; therefore, you must actively study God's Word and ask Him to give you wisdom and understanding of who He is and how He wants you to live out His Word every day. Like any other relationship, your relationship with God takes consistent communication, and He communicates ever-relevant truth and guidance through Scripture.

Love

God is perfectly clear concerning love—it's the fundamental requirement for a relationship with Him. Loving God is the greatest commandment, and loving others is the second. When it comes to love, He does not compromise. His expectation is abundantly clear in 1 John 4:7-8: "Beloved, let us love one another, for love is from God, and whoever loves has been born of God and knows God. Anyone who does not love does not know God, because God is love." You cannot love God without also loving people—*all* people.

Let's be honest—some people are hard to love. But if we all take a long, truly honest look in the mirror, we must admit we're all hard to love at times. Whether dealing with Christians or nonbelievers, loving people can be incredibly painful and challenging. As Christ followers, it's easy to say we love all people and want everyone to spend eternity in heaven, but our actions often speak louder when we struggle to speak kind words and perform selfless acts.

The flesh says love is a feeling, but if you've accepted Jesus, you know love is an action and a decision of the will that must be made every day. Loving others has nothing at all to do with who they are or what they deserve but has everything to do with who God is and what He's done for us. Not one of us has ever deserved God's love, but "God so loved the world, that he gave his only Son" (John 3:16). And if God—the King of Kings and Lord of Lords—loves us despite our sin, who are we to withhold love from others?

We live in a world where love is withheld on the basis of race, gender, socioeconomic status, political and religious affiliations, past mistakes, lifestyle choices, and just about any other excuse imaginable. It's as if differences and disagreements disqualify certain people from receiving love. We want to pick and choose whom to love based on the likelihood of their agreeing with us and loving us equally in return, yet we still struggle to love the people who agree with us and love us.

Loving some people will always be challenging because people are messy, but your ability to love like Jesus will become easier if you learn the "let it go" principle: Whatever happened, let it go. A friend betrayed your trust? Let it go. Someone gossiped about you behind your back? Let it go. You and a family member don't see eye to eye? Let it go. Most of what you fight over really doesn't matter from an eternal perspective, and holding on to it doesn't punish anyone but you. The more you choose to hold on to, the heavier your load to carry.

Yes, some circumstances and hardships will impact your life forever because of painful experiences with people, and the hardest thing to do is to extend forgiveness to a person who has hurt you but doesn't accept fault or apologize. But that doesn't mean you have to withhold forgiveness and love. Your ability to forgive isn't dependent on an apology. Jesus freely gave mercy and forgiveness that was undeserved, and we are expected to do the same—not for the other person but for us. We can't be right with God and at odds with people.

If we want God to work in our lives, we must extend love to others whether or not we think it's deserved. After all, we've never done anything to deserve God's love, yet He forgives us of all sin and has chosen to let it go. Who are we to operate under different standards for love? If we want love and forgiveness from God, we must willingly extend it to all of His children. As you'll recall, God helped me forgive my biological father for not being part of my life. I knew if God could forgive me, I could forgive him.

Our ultimate goal in life is to become like Jesus, but we will never become like Him until we strive to prioritize giving, obedience, God's Word, and love—daily. We cannot give, obey, surrender to God's authority, or love on our own. We must rely on the Holy Spirit to lead and guide us in the process—a lifelong process.

The plan and purpose for each of our lives is God-sized; therefore, our prayers should be for what only God can accomplish. He wants to defy the odds in your life, but you must believe Him for bigger. Don't settle for only what you can imagine. If you will believe Him for bigger and better things, He will do the unimaginable. What He's done for others, He will do for you! Your living in this time is no accident, and He has chosen *you* for even greater works.

A REVIVING BREATH OF HOPE

t's no secret that people all over the world are hurting, but you don't have to go far to find someone in need of hope and encouragement. Many people have been worn down by life's hardships and feel as if hope is dead.

In Ezekiel 37:4-6, the Lord brought Ezekiel to the middle of a valley filled with dry bones, then He instructed him,

> Prophesy over these bones, and say to them, O dry bones, hear the word of the LORD. Thus says the Lord GOD to these bones: Behold, I will cause breath to enter you, and you shall live. And I will lay sinews upon you, and will cause flesh to come upon you, and cover you with skin, and put breath in you, and you shall live, and you shall know that I am the LORD.

Ezekiel goes on to explain that he prophesied over those dry bones as the Lord commanded, and as he did, they began to rattle. Then they came together in flesh, received breath, and lived again. Those bones served as a representation for how Israel's hope had dried up. They were in need of a fresh filling to revive their hope in the Lord.

I'm convinced that people all over the world today are struggling with the same loss of hope Israel experienced. They have a desperate need for the hope of Christ to revive the dry bones scattered about the earth today. And just as God breathed life back into Israel, I believe He desperately wants to breathe life into our world today. I believe people need a breath of life and hope to bring revival to their dry jawbones, backbones, ankle bones, and "wishbones."

Jawbones

Romans 12:12 tells us to "rejoice in hope, be patient in tribulation, be constant in prayer." Many people need God to breathe life into their jawbones in order for their prayer lives to be transformed. When the troubles of life weigh you down, it becomes easy to pull away from God and withdraw from prayer. However, the only way you will be able to rejoice in hope and be patient in tribulation is through talking with God daily.

I pray that all of you reading this book will kneel at the feet of Jesus and lift your burdens to Him. The weight of your circumstances may be crushing the life out of you, but I pray a fresh breath of hope will bring revival to your jawbones and you will experience closeness with God through intimate prayer. Lay your burdens at His feet—He will comfort you like nothing in this world can.

Backbones

Just as the human backbone is responsible for strength and support, I pray that God will revive your spiritual backbone with His mighty breath of life. The backbone of your faith should be the Word of God. Hebrews 4:12 says, "The word of God is living and active, sharper than any two-edged sword." It's the strongest weapon against life's battles. You will cultivate hope in your heart when you allow God's Word to be the pillar of support and unwavering strength.

As you dig into Scripture, I pray God will make Himself known to you like never before and awaken your heart to the understanding of His deep love for you. While you may not have the answers for the many issues plaguing society, the Bible does. An answer for every situation can be found in God's Word. He doesn't want to keep anything secret from you, and He has already provided you with the compass to navigate through everything you will ever face. I pray God breathes life into the backbone of your faith through the awesome power of His Word and that hope overflows in your heart.

Ankle Bones

Adversity has a way of stopping you right in your tracks and leaving you fearful to make the next move. I pray that God will breathe life into your ankle bones so you can take steps toward obediently following wherever He leads. Don't let fear change your direction. Remain hopeful in the future God has planned for you!

I pray that you will step forward in confidence toward whatever God may be asking of you. You will never regret following Him, but you will most certainly regret telling Him no and missing out on fulfilling your purpose. May your response to God's calling be exactly as Ruth's when she said to her mother-in-law, "Where you go I will go" (Ruth 1:16). Never cease to follow God regardless of life's difficulties.

"Wishbones"

Over the course of life, most people hear the word *can't* significantly more than they hear the word *can*, which may be why so many struggle with self-esteem. When you're told *you can't* over and over, you can start to generally believe you can't. Then your tendency to dream big and believe God for great things will become nonexistent.

I pray that God will breathe a fresh breath of life into your "wishbone"! I pray He revives hope in you to believe that you are destined for greatness. After all, Jeremiah 32:17 says, "Ah, Lord God! It is you who have made the heavens and the earth by your great power and by your outstretched arm! Nothing is too hard for you." This should be your attitude concerning what God can do in your life—*nothing* is too hard for Him!

People desperate for hope too often seek it in all the wrong places. But hope can't be found in anything other than the mighty name of Jesus or you'll find yourself in the valley among the other dry bones.

Decide today that Jesus is enough and that He is your only hope for the future. Allow God to breathe life into your dry bones so you can live the life of abundance for which you were created.

Friend, I'm happy to report that as long as breath is in your lungs, God has a great plan for you. He's not finished with you yet, and He wants to use you in mighty ways. As you trust His good hand and follow where He leads, God will defy the odds in your life time and time again.

> *Dear Lord, I pray that all the individuals reading this book know just how much You love them. I pray You will build faith in their lives and let hope overflow from their hearts. I pray You will bless them indeed and, as Jabez asked of You, enlarge their borders. Defy the odds and use them greatly for Your kingdom. And may You receive all glory, honor, and praise for every good thing accomplished through each life. In the precious name of Jesus, amen.*

LEANING IN, DIGGING DEEPER

MY PRAYER OF HOPE AND TRUST IN THE LORD

NOTES

Introduction: The Need for Hope

1. A.W. Tozer, *The Pursuit of God: The Human Thirst for the Divine* (Chicago: Moody Publishers, 2015), 31.

2. Corrie ten Boom, Goodreads, https://www.goodreads.com/quotes/70125-never-be-afraid-to-trust-an-unknown-future-to-a.

Chapter 2: The Company You Keep

1. Henry Ford, Goodreads, https://www.goodreads.com/quotes/34931-my-best-friend-is-the-one-who-brings-out-the.

2. Charlie "Tremendous" Jones, *Tremendous Leadership*, https://tremendousleadership.com/pages/charlie.

Chapter 5: A Positive Perspective

1. Carey Kinsolving, "In a Fast-Food World, One Who Keeps the Faith," *The Washington Post*, July4,1992,https://www.washingtonpost.com/archive/local/1992/07/04/in-a-fast-food-world-one-who-keeps-the-faith/2bb5a876-4ba3-4482-adfd-d19d6879ec9b/.

2. Henry W. and Albert A. Berg Collection of English and American Literature, The New York Public Library, New York Public Library Digital Collections, https://digitalcollections.nypl.org/items/53b4cf90-7739-0132-f12c-58d385a7b928.

Chapter 6: Pray Miracle Prayers

1. William Carey, *Christianity Today*, Christian History, https://www.christianitytoday.com/history/people/missionaries/william-carey.html.

2. A.W. Tozer, *In Knowledge of the Holy: The Attributes of God* (North Fort Myers, FL: Faithful Life Publishers, 2014), 4.

Chapter 7: Persistence Got the Snail on the Ark

1. A.W. Tozer, *Man: The Dwelling Place of God* (Scots Valley CA: CreateSpace Independent Publishing Platform, 2017), 72.

2. "Don't Quit," *Virtues for Life*, https://www.virtuesforlife.com/poem-dont-quit/.

Chapter 8. Welcoming Weakness

1. Corrie ten Boom, *Goodreads*, https://www.goodreads.com/quotes/374714-you-may-never-know -that-jesus-is-all-you-need#:~:text=Quotes%20%3E%20Quotable%20Quote-,%E2%80%9C You%20may%20never%20know%20that%20JESUS%20is%20all%20you%20need, JESUS%20is%20all%20you%20have.%E2%80%9D.

Chapter 10: Embrace Change

1. Leah MarieAnn Klett, "Tommy Barnett on Most Important Thing He's Learned about Holy Spirit over Decades-Long Ministry," *The Christian Post*, April 19, 2020, https://www.christian post.com/news/tommy-barnett-on-most-important-thing-hes-learned-about-holy-spirit-over -decades-long-ministry.html.

2. Bruce Barton, *Goodreads*, https://www.goodreads.com/quotes/48173-when-you-re-through -changing-you-re-through.

3. "Want bigger plants? Get to the root of the matter," *ScienceDaily*, July 1, 2012, https://www.science daily.com/releases/2012/07/120701191636.htm.

4. Marti Trewe, "Business Advice from Babe Ruth That All Leaders Should Mind," *The American Genius*, February 4, 2019, https://theamericangenius.com/entrepreneur/business-advice-from -babe-ruth-that-all-leaders-should-mind/.

Chapter 11: Pray for the Desires of Your Heart

1. A.W. Tozer and James L. Snyder, *The Quotable Tozer: A Topical Compilation of the Wisdom and Insight of A. W. Tozer* (Minneapolis, MN: Bethany House, a division of Baker Publishing Group, 2018), 241.

Chapter 12: Believe God for Bigger

1. Dwight L. Moody, *Weighed and Wanting Addresses on the Ten Commandments*, chapter 3: "First Commandment" (San Antonio, TX: Bibliotech Press, 2020), 8.

2. Heather Clark, "2020 'State of the Bible' Report Finds Few Americans Read Bible Daily," *Christian News*, July 24, 2020, https://christiannews.net/2020/07/24/2020-state-of-the-bible -report-finds-few-americans-read-bible-daily/.

ACKNOWLEDGMENTS

To everyone who has inspired, supported, and encouraged me along the way: I am so grateful for each and every one of you. I always say if you see a turtle on a fence post, it didn't get there on its own, and I certainly didn't get here on my own.

To Savannah Abigail: You bring so much joy to me. I know it's been difficult being a sermon illustration your entire life, but I love you more than tongue can tell!

To Melba Williams (Mama): Thank you so much for the many sacrifices you made over the years. I greatly appreciate your constant love and support. I love you!

To Clayton Jones: You cared for our family when no one else did. Thank you for loving us and never giving up on us no matter how it might have affected your reputation.

To the Rock Springs Church Family: For all that has been accomplished at Rock Springs over the years, all glory be to God, the credit to you all, and the privilege has been all mine. Thank you for the happiest years of my life. I'm honored to be your pastor.

To the Rock Springs Church Staff: No one works harder than you. Every time you step to the plate, you knock the ball out of the park. Thank you for always being willing to do "whatever it takes" to reach people for Jesus. Thank you to Julie Pharr, my administrative assistant, who works tirelessly behind the scenes to keep things running smoothly.

To Brittany McKneely: Thank you for making Benny sound better!

To Johnny Hunt and James Merritt: To two of my dearest friends—thank you for sticking your necks out for me and believing in this book from the beginning. You both have been such an encouragement to me over the years.

To Bob Hawkins and the Harvest House Team: Thank you for taking a chance on me as an author. I am so grateful for this opportunity and for your insight and expertise throughout this process. Working with you has been a wonderful experience.

To Jesus Christ, my Lord and Savior: All glory, honor, and praise be to You alone. Thank You for using this ole boy from the wrong side of the tracks in ways I never could have imagined. I am in awe of all that You have done, and I can't wait to see what else You have in store!

ABOUT THE AUTHORS

Benny Tate, PhD, has served for more than 30 years as the senior pastor of Rock Springs Church in Milner, Georgia. Dr. Tate serves as president of the Congregational Methodist Church denomination, and he has served as chaplain for the United States Senate and the United States House of Representatives in Washington, DC, many times.

Brittany McKneely, staff writer at Rock Springs Church, worked as a high school English teacher for more than ten years before transitioning to full-time writing. She and her husband, Taylor, live in Georgia with their two wonderful boys. She and her family enjoy traveling the country and being outdoors.

CONNECTING WITH BENNY TATE

Stay engaged with

Defy the Odds

by visiting

DTObook.com

You can find
Pastor Benny Tate
on **Facebook**, **Instagram**,
and **Twitter**
by following:

@pastorbennytate

To learn more about Harvest House books and
to read sample chapters, visit our website:

www.harvesthousepublishers.com

HARVEST HOUSE PUBLISHERS
EUGENE, OREGON